George Smith Tyack

The Historic Dress of the Clergy

George Smith Tyack

The Historic Dress of the Clergy

ISBN/EAN: 9783744641142

Printed in Europe, USA, Canada, Australia, Japan

Cover: Foto ©ninafisch / pixelio.de

More available books at **www.hansebooks.com**

THE HISTORIC DRESS OF THE CLERGY.

The Cross, in Ritual, Architecture, and Art.

BY THE REV. GEO. S. TYACK, B.A.

Crown 8vo., 3s. 6d. Numerous Illustrations.

"This book is reverent, learned, and interesting, and will be read with a great deal of profit by anyone who wishes to study the history of the sign of our Redemption."—*Church Times*.

"An admirable and right-spirited book."—*The Churchwoman*.

"An exhaustive volume written in a thoroughly interesting and reliable manner, upon the manifold uses of the Cross, as the symbol of the Christian Faith. . . . The present volume will be valued by the Antiquary and the Churchman."—*Church Bells*.

"It is copiously and well illustrated, and lucidly ordered and written, and deserves to be widely known."—*Yorkshire Post*.

"The volume teems with facts, and it is evident that Mr. Tyack has made his study a labour of love, and spared no research, in order, within the prescribed limits, to make the work complete. He has given us a valuable work of reference, and a very instructive and entertaining volume."—*Birmingham Daily Gazette*.

"An engrossing and instructive narrative."—*Dundee Advertiser*.

"As a popular account of the Cross in history, we do not know that a better book can be named."—*Glasgow Herald*.

THE EMPEROR JUSTINIAN AND ARCHBISHOP MAXIMIANUS. *(From a Sixth Century Mosaic at Ravenna).*

Historic Dress

of the

Clergy, . . .

By the

Rev. Geo. S. Tyack, B.A.

LONDON:
WILLIAM ANDREWS & CO., 5, FARRINGDON AVENUE.

Preface.

IT is pleasing to observe on every hand signs of a lively, and growing, interest in things ecclesiastical. Subjects once left to the antiquary and the ecclesiologist, as requiring more time or learning than the claims of business would allow the mass of men to devote to them, are now studied by all classes with commendable earnestness and intelligence. It is to this general public that the author of the following pages addresses himself, in an attempt to supply, in a form popular yet exact, and brief yet comprehensive, an account of the historic dress of the clergy. His special aim has been to give useful information, and trustworthy help to the rank and file of the great and, he believes, daily growing forces of the English Church.

GEO. S. TYACK.

CROWLE, DONCASTER,
    March, 1897.

Contents.

PAGE

1. INTRODUCTION—Uniforms and class costumes—Interest in Clerical Dress—Levitical Vestments—Resemblances between Levitical and Christian Vestments—Civil origin of modern clerical Dress—Costume of Rome under the Empire—Principle of Vestments allowed—Colour of Primitive Church robes—Alleged use of Levitical sacerdotal insignia by Apostles—The robe of Macarius and the cloak of S. Paul—Results of primitive evidence as to Vestments 1

2. CASSOCKS AND COATS—Primitive use of the tunic and cloak—The philosophic habit—Rules concerning colours—Rise and influence of Monasticism—Effect of the conversion of Constantine—Result of the Barbarian invasion of Italy—Monastic habits adopted by clergy—Secularity of mediæval clergy in England and elsewhere—Influence of the Reformation—Puritans and Dissenters—Modern use of cassocks in England 13

3. COPES, CLOAKS, AND GOWNS—The *Paenula*—The *Pluvialis*—Secular copes—Canons' copes—The Ceremonial cope—Splendid Mediæval examples—Morses—Post-reformation use of the cope—The cope as a Eucharistic vestment—Gowns—Worn by the clergy out of doors—The "Preacher's Gown"—Dissenting and Scotch use of Gowns—The *Mandyas* ... 27

4. HEAD-GEAR—Hooded cloaks—The Almuce—Reason for its use—University Hoods—Canons concerning their use—The Square Cap—Development of the College Cap—The Biretta—Eastern Head-gear—Mitres—Early episcopal crowns—Development of the mitre—Abbatical and other non-episcopal mitres—Post-reformation use of Mitres in England—Cardinals' Hats—The Papal Tiara or *Regnum*—The Tonsure 40

CONTENTS.

5. LINEN AND LAWN—The Alb—Coloured and silken Albs—Apparels—Rubrics as to the Alb—Girdles—The Surplice—English surplices, ancient and modern—Puritan objections to it—The Cotta—The Rochet—Episcopal use of it—Continental developments of it—The Amice—Reason of its introduction—Silk Amices—White Ties and Bands   61

6. THE VESTMENT—Use of the term—The Chasuble—The *Casula* and *Planeta*—Ancient names for the Chasuble—Primitive shape and development of it—Splendid mediæval examples—Position in the English Prayer Book—The Dalmatic and the Tunicle—Secular Dalmatics—Introduction into the Church—The *Phaenolion*, *Polystaurion*, and *Sakkos*—The Stole—Its name and origin—Changes in its shape—Disuse and revival of the Stole in England—The *Orarion* and *Epitrachelion*—The Maniple—*Epimanicia*—The Humeral Veil   78

7. MISCELLANEA—Recapitulation of Vestments—The Bishop's Shoes—Use of Sandals and Boots—Gaiters—The Bishop's Gloves—Episcopal Rings—Pectoral Cross—The Archiepiscopal Pallium—Secular origin and early Shape—Modern form of it—Papal claims concerning it—The Rationale—The *succingulum* and *genuale*   107

8. COLOURS AND MYSTIC MEANINGS OF THE VESTMENTS—Primitive use of white—Introduction of Liturgical colours—The Roman sequence of colours—Old English sequences—Eastern use of colours—Meanings of the Vestments—Their Symbolic meaning—The Metaphorical meaning—Conclusion   118

Historic Dress of the Clergy.

CHAPTER I.

Introduction.

AS the world grows older, and the constitution of human society more intricate, the tendency to use a special kind of dress, a "uniform," to distinguish the various callings of men, seems to become increasingly strong. Amongst the professions, the Law (in its higher branches), the Army, and the Navy, as well as the Church, have long had their distinctive costumes. Medicine alone has assumed no special badge; and the reason is apparently one that touches the question at many points, namely, that the doctor alone of professional men exercises his art exclusively in private. Outside these professions we cannot fail to notice that almost every department of the public service, and even private undertakings when they arrive at such proportions as to make them of public importance, have in comparatively recent times adopted a uniform for their employées. The postal and telegraph services, the police and the commissionaires, the officers and men of our railway companies and the great shipping lines, these all illustrate the fact stated. We might go on to specify other divisions of modern society—

as for example, the department of Education, as illustrated by the quaint costume of the scholars of Christ's Hospital, the dress distinctive of Eton and other public schools, and the academic robes of the Universities,—but instances enough have been given to prove the popularity of what may be dubbed "class costume."

The history of the clerical dress claims a pre-eminence of interest for several reasons. The dignity of the order gives an importance to all that concerns its ministrations; controversy, theological and antiquarian, has made the subject a battle-ground; and, apart from these more or less debated points, it is beyond question the oldest illustration of that tendency in human society to which reference has been made. In days when the fashion of warriors' armour depended solely on personal taste and fancy, days ere navies had been formed, and when law and medicine had scarcely any existence apart from the Church, the vestments of ecclesiastics had long been regulated both by custom and by rule. Nay, we can go yet further back; for we have in the divinely ordered costume of the Levitical priesthood, if not the first instance in the world's history of a special dress for one order of society, at any rate the first detailed record of such a dress.

For this reason, as well as from the fact that efforts have been made in some quarters to trace an historical relation between the vestments of the Aaronic priesthood and those of the Christian Church, it will be fitting first of all to describe very briefly the sacred robes of the Jews.

The lowest order of the sacred ministers amongst the Israelites, the Levites, wore no distinguishing dress until the time of Agrippa; nor, except when engaged in the holy offices, were the higher orders differently clad from the rest of the people. The priests, however, wore during their ministrations four special garments, the linen breeches, the coat or tunic, the girdle, and the bonnet. The tunic was, like the sacred robe worn by our Saviour, woven throughout in one piece, and fitted closely to the body of the wearer. The girdle was the distinctive priestly vestment, and in its use is very suggestive of the Christian stole; it was worn round the back of the neck, crossed upon the breast, and then twisted round the body, with the ends hanging to the ground. The Rabbis, who seem to delight in exaggerating the size of the vestments of their priests, speak of it as being three fingers broad and sixteen yards long; it was, however, probably long enough for the ends to be gathered up and thrown over the shoulder, so as not to incommode the wearer, at the time of sacrifice. It was worn only during the actual ministration of the priestly office. The bonnet was a tall, peaked cap, "like the inverted calyx of a flower." These garments were all of linen, or, more strictly, of the snow-white "byssus," or cotton of Egypt. To these four vestments the high priest added four more, which were known as "golden vestments," from the fact that golden threads, together with the four colours consecrated to the use of the sanctuary, white, purple, blue, and scarlet, were woven into them. The *Meïl*, or robe, was of dark blue, and fell as far as the knees, the edge being adorned with pomegranates, worked in purple, blue, and scarlet, alternating with golden bells. The breast-plate was originally, according to the Rabbis, a kind of burse, or flat receptacle, stiffened in front with gold and jewels, in which were carried the mysterious Urim and Thummim; it was some ten inches square, and on the twelve gems set in the front were engraved the names of the tribes of Israel. In the later days of Jewish history, although the Urim and Thummim were not only lost, but the real import of their names was forgotten, the jewelled breast-plate was still worn by the high priest, attached by golden links to his shoulders, and by woven bands about his waist. The mitre was more splendid than the bonnet of the priest, and of greater height, attaining, according to the above-named absurd rabbinical exaggeration, the monstrous altitude of eight yards! Suspended from the mitre by a web of blue lace was the *Ziz*, or frontlet, a golden plate two fingers wide and the length of the forehead, on which was engraved "Holiness to the Lord."

Any office performed by high-priest, or priest, without all the vestments of his order was deemed to be invalid; and when the vestments were soiled, they were not washed, but used for making wicks for the lamps of the sanctuary. The high priest had a complete new set for the Great Day of Atonement in each year.

It will at once be recognised that a certain similarity in appearance may be traced between most of these vestments and those now worn by the clergy throughout the greater part of Christendom. The Jewish priest in his linen tunic girded about him as just described, would bear some resemblance to him of to-day in alb and girdle and crossed stole; while any one of the more ornate vestments of the Christian Church, the cope, the chasuble, or (still more clearly) the dalmatic, might be suggested by the splendid robe of the high priest, whose tall bonnet and breast-plate might also seem to foreshadow the episcopal mitre and the pectoral cross.

Mere resemblance of form, however, may be as delusive a guide to the derivation of things as mere likeness in sound has often proved in tracing the origin of words; and therefore, to prevent misapprehension, it will be well before going further to state clearly that no ecclesiologist of note now contends for the derivation of the Christian vestments from Jewish originals. A few points of similarity between the two may be found on comparison; but it is agreed that these are either accidental, or possibly, in one or two cases, have arisen from an attempt made in mediæval times to render vestments already in use somewhat analogous to those of the earlier dispensation.

In fact it is now generally admitted by all ecclesiastical antiquaries that the dress of the clergy of the primitive Church did not differ in shape or in material from that worn by the laity, except that in their ministrations they assumed garments such as it was usual for Roman gentlemen to wear on solemn or festive occasions.

The situation in which the Church was placed during the first three centuries rendered such a custom unavoidable. For the bishops and priests of the Church to have gone abroad in a garb that at once marked them out as leaders of the Christians would have been an act of folly in days when bitter persecution was constantly threatening, even when not actually rife. For the origin of the dress of the clergy, then, we must examine that worn by persons of position in the first century.

The most commonly used garment of those times was the *chiton*, or tunic, a dress which fitted fairly closely to the body, and had short sleeves. It varied in length, sometimes reaching to the ankles, sometimes barely covering the knees, and in ordinary cases was probably of some serviceably dark tint. It was frequently ornamented with two stripes running down the front from either side of the neck,—stripes which differed in breadth and perhaps in colour, according to the dignity of the wearer, a senator for instance, using a broad *clavus* (as it was called) a knight a narrower one. In early frescoes this striped tunic is often seen, suggesting a striking resemblance to the surplice and black stole of a modern Anglican clergyman. The resemblance, however, as we shall see, is in no sense historical. Such a garment is seen in the illustration representing a fresco in one of the catacombs of Rome ; an aged man is seated on a chair, while before him stand two youths clad in tunics adorned with clavi. This has sometimes been described as a representation of an early confirmation, but there is good reason for doubting if this be correct. All that concerns our present purpose is to mark the dresses of the three persons, two of whom, at any rate, are intended for laymen.

On occasions of state a Roman gentleman wore over this tunic a long and ample robe, the *toga*. This, at one time the characteristic dress of every adult Roman citizen, must from its nature have been almost always laid aside when any exertion was required, as in toil or travel ; but more than this, it had in the first century of our era been dropped altogether by the lower orders. It held its place, however, as the recognized form of court dress, to be worn by all who were received by the Emperor, and as the appropriate habit for civil or religious ceremonial. The advocate wore it when pleading in the forum, it was seen at public sacrifices, in a white toga the dead were carried to their "long home," and the mourners followed in togas of black. In the eyes of the world, therefore, there was one form of dress, which, though not confined to the use of the priests, was considered specially suitable for solemn occasions; and it was by the use of this that the early Church was able to express her sense of the dignity of her sacred rites without exciting the notice or the attacks of the heathen populace.

There is reason to suppose, moreover, that the principle underlying the use of sacred vestments—the setting aside of certain garments for exclusive employment in the holy mysteries—was from the first evident. The toga and tunic used at the altar became sacred things, to be worn henceforth for no other purposes. To this intent S. Jerome, writing in the fourth century, but evidently expressing the feeling prevalent throughout the Church, speaks, "We ought not to go into the sanctuary just as we please, and in our ordinary clothes, defiled with the visage of common life, but with clear conscience and clean garments handle the sacraments of the Lord."

FROM THE CATACOMBS.

A further point of distinction in the garments worn in sacred ministrations, and perhaps also in the secular robes of the Christian clergy, was the restriction of the colour to white, the stripes upon the tunic being probably black. In this the Church was influenced by the ideas of purity and gladness, so naturally suggested by that colour, and also probably by a prevalent impression, with which, as we have seen, the vestments of the old dispensation coincide, that white was peculiarly appropriate to the service of the Deity. In proof of this we may once more quote S. Jerome who in his work against the Pelagians, demands "What is there, I ask, offensive to God, if I wear a tunic more than ordinarily handsome, or if Bishop, Priest, and Deacon, and other ministers of the Church, in the administration of the sacrifices come forth in white clothing?" Hegesippus, a Jew, who about the year 180, became a convert to Christianity, tells us that S. James the Just, the first bishop of Jerusalem, when he was about "to offer supplication for the people," was accustomed to "use garments, not of wool, but of linen."

Two ancient writers seem to imply that at any rate some of the Apostles adopted part of the distinctive vestments of the Jewish high-priest, to mark the analogous position to which they had been called in the new dispensation. Polycrates of Ephesus, writing as early as the close of the second century, speaks of S. John "becoming a priest, wearing the golden plate." As all tradition avers that S. John the Divine became the first bishop of Ephesus, and died there early in the second century, the evidence of Polycrates, also an Ephesian, and almost a contemporary, is especially valuable. Epiphanius, bishop of Constantia, or Salamis, in

Crete from the year 367 to 403, gives similar testimony concerning S. James. "It was permitted him," so he says, "to wear the golden plate upon his head;" and he refers to Eusebius and to S. Clement as supporting the statement. It is, perhaps, well to note that Epiphanius was by birth a Jew of Palestine, so that he may be supposed to have been familiar with the local tradition on the subject.

A passage in Theodoret, who was born about 393, and became bishop of Cyrus in Syria in 420, has often been quoted to prove the early use of distinctive ecclesiastical vestments, but too much stress should not be placed on it. It is to the effect that the Emperor Constantine gave to Macarius, bishop of Jerusalem, a sacred robe, woven of gold thread, for him to wear when administering holy baptism. The passage does not, however, necessarily imply that the robe was specially suitable for its sacred purpose in any other respect than in its splendour; and when Theodoret goes on to inform us that S. Cyril of Jerusalem was charged with having sold the robe, and that a stage dancer had bought and used it, it seems probable that it did not differ in fashion from secular clothing.

From all this it will be obvious that there is still less evidence to support the contention of those who would seek proof of a primitive use of sacerdotal vestments in S. Paul's message in his second epistle to S. Timothy;—"The cloak that I left at Troas with Carpus, when thou comest, bring with thee, and the books, but especially the parchments." In fact the attempt to make a chasuble out of this cloak is distinctly a modern one. Tertullian, in his treatise on prayer, refers to the passage. He notes a heathen custom of removing the cloak during prayer, a practice which he counts among "empty observances," not to be insisted on as if they were founded on divine precept or apostolical command, of which there is no evidence; "unless indeed," he sarcastically adds, "any one should think that it was in prayer that Paul threw off his cloak and left it with Carpus." Tertullian here treats the cloak as a garment which might conceivably be put off for divine worship, certainly not as one to be specially put on for the purpose. S. Chrysostom in one of his Homilies, speaks to the same effect, evidently regarding the cloak as an ordinary garment merely.

Two conclusions, then, appear to be obviously deducible from the evidence of the primitive ages concerning the dress of the clergy. First, that in their public ministrations ecclesiastics wore garments not different in shape from those used on certain occasions by the civil society around them; and in their everyday life, garments differing in material and in colour no more than in form. For this we have seen an obvious reason in the persecution which raged continually about the Church during her earliest years. An exact parallel to such a state of things was supplied in our own country, so far as the ordinary dress is concerned, by the Roman Catholic clergy, who mixed among their scattered flocks during the reigns of the later Stuarts in lay attire, in consequence of the severe penal laws enacted against them. To this reason we may, no doubt, add another, when we recollect the poverty of the primitive Church, which made the provision of any costly accessories to public worship well nigh impossible.

Our second conclusion is, that, in spite of this, the principle underlying the use of a special garb, at least at the time of ministration, was both felt and acknowledged, so far as circumstances allowed. The clergy, while officiating, wore the dress which society recognized as appropriate for solemn ceremonial, and in colour that which was esteemed specially befitting divine worship; and they gave to this garb almost the character of a vestment, by reserving it exclusively for sacred purposes. Due weight must also be given to the evidence proving the use, at least by some of the Apostles, of distinctly sacerdotal insignia.

From this dignified costume of imperial Rome, has been evolved throughout the centuries the sacerdotal dress of the clergy of the Church of mediæval and modern times, and, for the most part, even that fashion of attire which is recognized as distinctive of their order in common life; an attire, in the use of which, "the ministers of all denominations" have almost universally, in England, imitated the example of the ecclesiastics.

The controlling influence in this development has been that conservatism which naturally arises from the regard which all devout men must feel for the customs of their forefathers in religious matters; a conservatism intensified in this case by a sense of the impropriety which would be shown by the Church, if she followed the frequent changes of the fickle fashions of the world. Thus, while the world altered and re-altered the cut of its clothes from the mere passion for novelty, the Church, from a reverential regard for antiquity, kept so far as possible to the older forms, and only with great deliberation came to modify the clerical dress, yielding slowly, as if under protest, to the influence of circumstances. At times of violent upheaval and commotion, when the reins of discipline are slack, and individual caprice can venture to assert itself, changes have sometimes been initiated which have left their mark when peace has been restored ; on the other hand, we find large tracts of time scarcely marked by change of any kind. From this point of view, also, the history of clerical dress has its interest. Comparatively unimportant as the cut of a coat, or the colour of a vestment may be, such things have, from time to time, illustrated the drift of thought on other and more vital matters.

One further conclusion follows necessarily from the facts already adduced, facts, it may be well to say here, whose existence is now acknowledged by all competent ecclesiologists, no matter to what part of the Church they may belong. A mystical meaning is now attached to each vestment, especially to those worn at the offering of the Eucharist, and of this the priest is reminded by the appropriate prayer appointed to be said as each is donned. It will be obvious that if these vestments have been historically developed from such originals as have been described, these meanings must be an afterthought. Excellent and edifying as they are, the moral and spiritual lessons which are now suggested to the priest as he prepares himself for the altar, have been drawn by the pious fancy of devout men in past times from robes adopted originally for quite different reasons.

CHAPTER II.

Cassocks and Coats.

THE ordinary dress of a priest, as we have seen, was in the first century a sleeved tunic which might vary in length, reaching either to the knees or to the ankles, according probably to the taste of the wearer. In early frescoes in Rome several examples may be found. In the cemetery of S. Agnes is a representation of our Lord seated amid six of the apostles; all are clad in the long tunic, with a clavus, or dark stripe, by way of ornament, that on the Saviour's tunic being broader than the others. And in the cemetery of S. Hermes, in a fresco supposed to be as late as the time of Pelagius II., pope from 578 to 590, we have an ideal ordination of a deacon, where the deacon wears a short tunic, and the other figures, probably intended for our Lord seated on a throne, and two of the apostles, wear long ones, together with the toga.

When an upper garment was needed for secular wear, a short cloak, called a birrus, or byrrhus, was used; and clad in this S. Cyprian went forth to martyrdom in the year 258. A tendency, however, early showed itself to adopt instead of this the more dignified and wider pallium with the long tunic, as worn by the student and the philosopher. It was the dress of the men of thought rather than of the men of action, to whose limbs the shorter and less ample attire gave greater freedom. Heraclas, a priest and afterwards Bishop of Alexandria, having been numbered amongst the philosophers, continued to wear the pallium after taking orders, as Eusebius testifies; and S. Jerome says the same of his friend Nepotian. Others, however, who had not studied in the schools of philosophy, sought to lay claim to superior devotion, or perhaps to intimate superior wisdom, by donning the philosopher's habit with its cloak of rough wool. To check this the Council of Gangra in 325 passed a canon condemning every one who "used the pallium, or cloak, upon the account of an ascetic life; and, as if there were some holiness in that, condemned those that wore the birrus and other garments that are commonly employed." In a similar spirit S. Celestine, Pope of Rome from 423 to 432, wrote to reprimand some of the clergy of Gaul.

As regards colour, from the first there was a prejudice in favour of the white of the undyed material. "With reason, as it seems to me," exclaims S. Clement of Alexandria, "did they act, who held scents and unguents in such disesteem, that they banished the compounders of them from well-regulated states, and in nowise differently dealt with the dyers of wools." And yet more plainly he says: "For men of hearts pure and uncontaminated, a white and simple garb is the most fitting." In imperial Rome, where the nobles flashed and flaunted in scarlet and purple and gold, and the long trains of their clients and slaves were scarcely less gorgeous in their trappings, we may easily imagine that white attire, far from being the conspicuous object which it would be with us, would appear simple and modest. Yet the great practical advantage of a darker hue for everyday use would doubtless have its influence then as now, and white seems not to have been universally adopted by the Christian clergy.

Several councils, as that at Carthage in 348, and another at Agde in 506, warn the clergy to wear only such garments as are suitable to their profession, but give no detailed direction on the matter. S. Jerome, writing to Nepotian, distinctly advises him to wear neither black nor white, the one suggesting an ostentatious seriousness, and the other a fastidious delicacy. Probably custom in such a matter differed in different places. At Constantinople, in the days of S. Chrysostom, the clergy wore black. A white pallium, however, came to be regarded as a proper robe for a bishop, especially if he ruled over an important see. Thus S. Chrysostom himself wore white, as did S. Cyril; while it was his lack of regard for the usual dignity of archiepiscopal dress, as he himself says, that helped to stir up the ill-feeling of Constantinople against S. Gregory Nazianzen.

In the fourth and fifth centuries several events took place which had considerable influence on the dress of the clergy. Monasticism took its rise from the example of S. Anthony the Hermit; Constantine came to the imperial throne and made Christianity the religion of the state; and in the first years of the fifth century the tide of northern barbarism—Goths, Vandals, and Lombards—began to break across the Alps and sweep the plains of Italy and of the whole of Southern Europe.

S. Anthony gathered about him a company of devout souls, who in the remote deserts of the Thebaid set themselves to live a life of discipline, self-denial, and labour. The movement spread with wonderful rapidity. The founder is said to have seen five thousand followers about him before his death; and his disciples Amatha and Macarius established new communities elsewhere, in

Egypt, and in Syria Eugenius carried the custom to Mesopotamia, and Hilarion to Palestine; S. Athanasius, driven from Alexandria by Arian persecution in 341, introduced monasticism to the people of Italy, and from thence S. Martin of Tours carried it to France, and S. Augustine of Hippo to the province of North Africa. Thus within a century the Christian world was overspread by the devout and earnest enthusiasm of the early hermits and monks.

These recluses made no claim, as such, to a share of the clerical authority, yet the influence of men, vowed to a religious life, could not but be felt by the appointed teachers of religion. This influence was immeasurably strengthened when the bishops began to ordain monks as priests or deacons. Their ascetic habits of life and dress would unquestionably work like leaven among the secular clergy, as in every movement, those whose convictions are most definite, and whose line of conduct is most clearly marked, are sure to take the lead. In shape there was probably little difference between the clothes worn by the monks in the deserts, and by the clergy and laity in the towns; but the now universal custom among clergymen, of wearing dark, if not black, clothes, is very likely due to the habits of those ancient anchorites. The monastic tunic was rough, and of a dark colour, sometimes made of hair-cloth, sometimes of a shaggy skin, in imitation of S. John Baptist, the pattern for hermits, who wore a raiment of camel's hair. The ideas of penitence, of devotion, of occupation in holy things—in all of which the primitive recluses were pre-eminent—thus early connected themselves with dark clothing, as a seemly setting for a thoughtful soul; and the connection has remained. Sulpicius Severus assures us that S. Martin wore the monastic dress, and it is reasonable to suppose that he was not alone in thus adopting it.

The conversion of Constantine, and the subsequent recognition of the Church by the State, had an influence affecting almost all departments of the Church's outward life. The last rumble of the thunder of general persecution had rolled away; the sky was clear, and hopeful of a bright future. Christian men were able openly to display the emblems of their faith, and the clergy were no longer shepherds carrying their own lives in their hands, while they watched and tended a harried flock. There remained no reason why bishop and priest should not be openly known as such. The opportunity for the clergy to become thus marked off from the world, was provided by an event which seems to have little relation to such things, namely, the barbarian invasion of Italy.

It was in the year 408 that this incursion of the North into the South began, and, by the end of the sixth century, it had created a perfect revolution in the manners and customs of the Roman world. Among other changes, the long and ample robes which dignified the citizens of the imperial city were abandoned, and a tunic and cloak (the *cottus* and *sagum*), of even smaller proportions than those formerly worn by the working classes of the metropolis, came into vogue. The bustling, practical North had imposed upon the South a costume fitted for war and the chase, for journeys and all active exercise, but lacking those marks of repose and of almost sovereign dignity, which even the poorest Roman citizen had formerly claimed by virtue of his citizenship.

It is here that we meet with the first instance of that conservatism in the Church, of which mention has been made; for now, for the first time, the clergy were to be distinguished from the laity in point of dress, from the mere fact that, while all the world changed its fashion, the Church maintained her ancient usages.

S. Gregory the Great, who ascended the pontifical throne in 590, would tolerate no one about him who wore the garb of the barbarians, and throughout his writings he constantly assumes that a distinctive form of clerical dress was known and accepted at that time; the clergy must not, he says in one place, "behave otherwise in conduct than they profess in their dress."

Abundant evidence is forthcoming from this period of the recognition of the change which had taken place. The fourth Council of Constantinople (the Council in Trullo), meeting in 691, has a canon directed against those priests who, either in their parishes or when travelling, wore robes different from those prescribed. A council at Soissons, in 744, forbade the clergy the use of the short, military, *sagum*, and prescribes the long cloak, which it calls *casula*. These two examples will be sufficient to indicate the prevailing feeling of the time, both in the East and the West.

The fathers of the Church, at about the same era, began to regulate the colour as well as the shape of clerical attire. A council at Narbonne, in 589, prohibits the clergy from wearing purple, on the ground, it is alleged, that the barbarians especially affected that colour. And again, an Eastern Council, the second of Nicæa, in 787, passed canons against ecclesiastics arraying themselves in rich and brilliant colours.

During all this time, the monastic system was spreading even more widely, and becoming allied with yet closer intimacy to the clerical life. S. Benedict, who died in 542, promulgated that great rule of life, which, as it superseded all previous efforts to introduce system into the monasteries of the West, so also has been the foundation of every subsequent endeavour. The first English abbey was founded by S. Columban in 563, Bangor had a community of three hundred monks in 603, and S. Benedict Biscop built the twin monasteries of Yarrow and Bishop Wearmouth in 677.

The ancient dress of the monks was a linen sleeveless tunic (the *colobion*), a goat-skin habit with a cowl, and a long black cloak. This last was the *casula*, a covering worn by peasants and the poor to protect themselves from wet or cold; and for this reason adopted by the monks, under vows of poverty and humility, in preference to any more handsome robe. S. Augustine tells a story of an old man, "very pious and poor," who had lost his casula, and we read of Fulgentius, Bishop of Ruspa, about the year 507, and of S. Cæsarius, Archbishop of Arles, in 540, both men conspicuous for their saintly poverty, wearing cloaks of the same kind.

The use of this dress became so far general among the clergy, that it came to be regarded as the most fitting and proper outdoor attire; and thus, in 742, we find S. Boniface decreeing that "priests and deacons are not to use *saga* (short cloaks), like the laity, but *casulæ*, like servants of God."

By the eighth century, therefore, it seems that we may conclude that the standard of the ordinary secular dress of the clergy had become to a large extent fixed, framed on the model which the primitive monks had assumed from their desire for humble simplicity. The long tunic and the cowled cloak, both probably of a dark colour, would thus be the common clerical costume.

The accompanying representations of an Augustinian and of a Cistercian monk, will illustrate the style of costume assumed, with some variations, by all the different orders. In the canons of S. Augustine we have the oldest of the monastic orders; their habit consisting of a black cassock and cloak, with a girdle and a cape or hood. Many other religious bodies, whose rules and habits vary in some respects, are derived from the Augustinian order. The Cistercians also, for the most part, wear black, although white is permitted in choir. So far as the monastic habit concerns the clerical, the several garments other than the cassock, which these figures illustrate, will be noticed in subsequent pages.

CANON OF S. AUGUSTINE.

Individual eccentricity or vanity will, however, at all times assert itself; it is not therefore surprising that councils and synods found it needful again and again to check attempts at personal display. A council at Melfi, near Naples, in 1086, condemned a custom that was growing up of wearing cloaks cut away in front. The French clergy were forbidden, by a synod at Albi, in 1254, to use long sleeves; and by another at Paris, to wear clothes of several colours. The attempt to gain uniformity was not, however, very successful at first, and as time went on there was a growing tendency to assimilate once more the dress of ecclesiastics to that of laymen. Councils at Cologne and elsewhere struggled manfully against this secularity in the priesthood, and from some of their decrees we gather that in the thirteenth century the clergy sometimes wore clothes of red or green, and trimmed with costly furs.

In these respects the English Clergy were no better than their foreign brethren. A synod in London, in 1268, "ordained and strictly charged that no clergyman should wear garments ridiculous or remarkable for shortness, but reaching to below the middle of the leg . . . and that they wear close capes, except when travelling." Another synod at Lambeth followed in the same strain in 1287; yet in 1343 another London synod complains of priests wearing short, wide coats with long, hanging sleeves which leave the elbows bare; and the subject crops up once more at Salisbury, in 1420.

CISTERCIAN MONK.

The illuminated manuscripts of the Middle Ages constantly represent ecclesiastics arrayed in the gayest of colours, and in garments adorned with gold and jewels and costly furs. John Wynd-hill, the rector of Arncliffe, bequeathed by will, in 1431, two green gowns, another of murrey, and a fourth of sanguine silk, together with two more of black, all of them trimmed with fur; also a girdle of sanguine silk, and a second green and white, both adorned with silver gilt; and yet another girdle of silver. Other wills made by priests at about that time are full of similar details; green, crimson and purple gowns, girdles enriched with the precious metals, and even daggers with carved ivory handles, and other costly items of personal dress are not uncommon legacies among the clergy. Indeed, so regularly were bright colours in use, that at York, in the year 1519, it was found advisable even in respect to funerals to specially point out the seemliness of wearing black. "We thynke it were convenient," the presentation runs, "that whene we fetche a corse to the churche, that we shoulde be in our blak abbettes (habits) morningly, w^t our hodes of the same of our hedes, as is used in many other places."

The canons of synods and councils, referred to above, sufficiently attest the mind of the Church on this matter; but it is evident that the popular conscience was not shocked by the prevailing gaiety of clerical costume.

The Greek Church succeeded in establishing the universal use of black garments by her ecclesiastics as early as the tenth century. It took a longer time to establish the custom in the West, and black was not the general use in France until the fifteenth century, nor in Italy until the sixteenth. Since then, the ordinary dress of the continental clergy has not altered in anything, beyond small and insignificant details; the black cassock being the universal attire, although its shape may have small local differences. Monastic or regular clergy wear, of course, the habit of their order, which may be, as with the Premonstratensians, white in colour, or, as with others, brown or grey. Bishops, however, are distinguished by the use of purple, and Cardinals by scarlet; the Pope wears a white cassock.

In England, the last three hundred years have witnessed many changes, owing to the feeling engendered first at the Reformation period, and then at the time of Puritan ascendancy.

In 1551, Hooper, Bishop of Gloucester, found it needful in his Injunctions to ask,—"Whether they (the parish priests) go in sober, modest, and comely apparel, without any cuts, jags, or such like external and undecentness not to be used in our ministers of the Church." In 1571, Grindal, Archbishop of Canterbury, made a "Metropolitical Visitation" of his province, and had to enquire even concerning cathedral dignitaries, "Whether they use seemly or priestly garments, according as they are commanded by the Queen's Majesty to do." The command referred to is undoubtedly the injunction issued under Elizabeth to the effect that the clergy should wear "such seemly habits, garments, and square caps as were most commonly and orderly received in the later year of King Edward VI.;" and the reason is given as follows,—"that they should be had as well in outward reverence as otherwise regarded for the worthiness of their ministries, and thinking it necessary to have them known to the people in all places and assemblies, both in the Church and without."

The Puritans, however, were eager for the rejection of every kind of specially clerical apparel, and pressed some rather original arguments into their service. Thomas Cartwright, the Puritan leader, and the antagonist of Archbishop Whitgift, in seeking to prove that no such distinction of dress was made in Scriptural times, does not appeal to those facts with which, as we have seen, history might have supplied him, but urges that Samuel the prophet was unrecognised by Saul until he declared himself, that our Lord was known to His enemies only by the kiss of Judas, and that S. Peter revealed his discipleship, not by his clothes, but by his Galilean brogue.

Calvin, however, held that the prophets of the Old Testament were "known from other men by a certain and peculiar form of cloak," and that therefore "doctors," or teachers, might reasonably differ from others in dress, so long as they kept to gravity and modesty. Hooker found it necessary to defend the use of clerical dress in his "Ecclesiastical Polity." He treats the matter as really of small moment, yet maintains that, in the face of the custom of "all well-ordered polities," "it argueth a disproportioned mind in them whom so decent orders displease."

The dissenters from the first rejected all such distinctions in clothing, but the cassock remained the recognised dress of the clergy. As time passed on, however, the cassock began to undergo considerable modification for secular use. It was cut shorter till it barely reached the knees; the girdle or cincture formerly worn with it ceased to be needful for so curtailed a garment, and was discarded; and finally the cassock was allowed to hang unbuttoned save at the throat. And thus the clerical coat of to-day was gradually evolved; and to the use of that the dissenters of the latter part of the nineteenth century have taken as eagerly, and almost as unanimously, as their forefathers protested against it in its proper form.

The seventy-fourth canon of the English Church (issued in 1604), enjoins "decency of apparel" upon "ministers."

It prescribes that in public they should use a "coat or cassock," and "that they wear not any light-coloured stockings." This last homely injunction had its obvious reason in days when trunk-hose were worn beneath a cassock sufficiently short for comfortable walking, and it reminds us that the knee-breeches and gaiters, now often considered specially characteristic of the secular attire of dignitaries such as bishops and archdeacons, is in reality simply the survival of what was once the proper dress of all the clergy.

The use of the cassock had in the early part of the present century, well-nigh dropped out of use in England with the ordinary parish priests; although its use together with gown and bands by court-chaplains, university preachers, and as the requisite court-dress of ecclesiastics other than bishops (who on such occasions wear rochet and chimere) still gave evidence of its official propriety. The revival of its employment, as one of the minor outward signs of the progress of the Catholic revival of the last half century, was at one time a mark of adherence to High Church teaching. It is now once more in general use in the public service of the church; but it is well to point out that the cassock is in no sense a vestment, in the technical acceptation of that word. It is, merely the orthodox form of the clerical coat, over which the robes and vestments proper to the divine offices are worn. To put it on as is commonly done in England now, with the surplice or other robes merely for church use, is a more seemly and dignified practice than entirely to discard it; but, nevertheless, such a custom undoubtedly puts the cassock into a position amongst clerical garments which it was not intended to occupy.

The revived orders of mission priests, such as the Society of S. John (the "Cowley Fathers,") and the Society of S. Paul, have naturally and logically taken to the full use of the cassock in daily life amongst their members; and the clergy of some English parishes have followed the example thus set. That it is the historical and dignified costume worn by all the clergy of this country down to comparatively recent times, cannot be denied.

CHAPTER III.

Copes, Cloaks, and Gowns.

SOME of the earlier ground on which the history of copes and capes is established has already been unavoidably travelled, in considering that dress of imperial Rome which circumstances have made to be the original model of almost all clerical attire; for the cope, like the chasuble of which we must speak hereafter, is probably derived from the *paenula*, a cloak nearly related in shape to the casula.

The paenula was a large "over-all," without sleeves, and furnished with a hood, which might be turned up over the head as an additional protection in tempestuous weather. Originally it was to some extent a humble dress, standing distinct from the dignified toga of Roman citizenship, and from the *chlamys*, or short cloak, of the soldier. From its convenience, however, as a defence against both cold and rain, it came to be regarded as a suitable garment for travellers, yet it still remained so far unfashionable that it was necessary for the Emperor Alexander Severus (222-235 A.D.) to give special permission before it was thought right for senators to wear it within the city, even in inclement weather. A couple of centuries later the paenula had become the usual upper garment of residents in Rome, taking the place of the more graceful and historic toga.

The original character of the cope in ecclesiastical use is sufficiently indicated by its early name of *pluvialis*, or rain-cloak. It is, in fact, said to have been introduced amongst the clergy by Pope Stephen, in 256, as a garment to be worn in the outdoor portion of their functions, as in processions, and at funerals.

Some relics of the secular origin of the cope long clung to it, and indeed, still remain. As late as the thirteenth and fourteenth centuries it was a wide cloak forming part of the secular attire of the clergy; and, as such, it was from time to time tampered with in shape, colour, and adornment, in a way which brought vigorous condemnation from the provincial synods. Secular copes of red and green are mentioned, sometimes with sleeves added to them, trimmed round the edge with fringes or with furs; in some cases slashed open up the sides, in others, buttoned down the front. But even in its use in divine service the cope shows its origin, in the fact that it has never become an exclusively sacerdotal vestment. In the choir offices—the services sung in the choir at the canonical hours—it was the custom in mediæval times for all the "clerks" (clergy of whatever degree) to wear over their surplices black stuff copes. The fact that this rule was universal as regards the night hours, while at the offices of the day hours this funereal garment was discarded only during the summer at the highest festivals, namely from Easter to Michaelmas, points distinctly to the idea that it was worn, not as a vestment, but as a warm cloak. The Sarum rule thus speaks of this use: "Concerning the dress and condition of the Clerks who come into choir; of whatever rank they be, we ordain that they have decent black copes, at least to their heels, with surplices not exceeding their copes in length." Similiar rules obtained at S. Paul's in London, at Exeter, and indeed throughout the dioceses of England, Scotland, and Ireland, and in those of Northern France. This black robe was known as a canon's cope, from its use by the canons, or regular clergy.

In the course of time this cope got to be contracted more and more in breadth, until it became a broad band only, generally of black silk, which, under the name of a canon's, or a chaplain's, scarf, has lasted to our day.

The original purpose of the cope is also suggested by its shape. Being intended mainly for use out of doors, it was provided, as above pointed out, with a hood. As it became more nearly allied to the recognised vestments in its uses, and was thus worn with increasing frequency within the Church, the need of the hood became less pressing, and when other forms of head-gear, such as caps, came into use in the Church, the hood ceased to have any other purpose than that of ornament. It still remains, however, a semi-circular, or shield-shaped appendage to the back of the cope, as a witness to the earlier custom.

On festivals, the higher clergy wore copes of richer material in choir. The clergy having the control of the music, whether at the daily offices or at the Holy Eucharist, and named from the duty Rulers of the Choir, wore silk copes, and there are notices in ancient inventories and elsewhere of these special cantors' copes. Leofric, Bishop of Exeter from 1046 to 1072, gave to his Cathedral three "Cantercappae;" and Bishop John de Grandison (1328-1370) gave three more. S. Margaret, Queen of Scotland, gave amongst other vestments "Chanters' copes" to some of the churches in that country.

Finally it came to pass that the cope was regarded as the proper robe for the officiant at all solemn services other than the Eucharist. It is used for processions, whether within the church or without, at Evensong when sung with special solemnity, at the administration of Holy Baptism on great and special occasions, at Benediction, and at the solemnity of the Asperges, or sprinkling of Holy Water preparatory to the Eucharist. A bishop wears it also at the pontifical offices of Ordination, Confirmation, the Consecration of Churches, and on other similar occasions. At these times its colour depends upon the festival, or the office at which it is worn.

At the same time the lay use of the cope has not quite disappeared. The robe of state worn by an English peer is simply a cope, developed upon very slightly different lines; and a cope forms also part of the coronation robes of most European sovereigns.

In almost all ages and places the out-door coat of the clergy for cold or wet weather has taken a wide and flowing form, rather than a close-fitting one. A priest's cloak, both in the East and in the West, has to this day maintained to a great extent the shape of the original pluvialis. Adorned and beautified till it has become one of the most gorgeous of the vestments of the Church, that cloak of old Rome has at the same time developed in another and simpler manner, into a modern, as it was an ancient, overcoat.

The present shape of a cope is a wide semi-circle, the straight side of which goes round the neck and falls to the feet in front, the curved side forming the bottom right round the wearer. Behind is the hood, already referred to, which is often ornately embroidered and jewelled; and it is fastened by a morse, or clasp, in front. So handsome were some of the mediæval morses that in inventories of Church vestments they are catalogued separately from the copes. In the S. Paul's inventory of 1295 mention is made of morses of gold and silver enriched with jewels; and again in a Sarum inventory of 1222 there are others equally splendid. For the further adornment of these costly vestments they frequently have broad bands of velvet, or other material, called orfrays (or orphreys) running along the straight edge which falls in front in two lines.

The number and magnificence of the copes which accumulated in the Cathedrals and great Abbey Churches of England in the middle ages is almost incredible. At Canterbury, in 1315, were more than sixty copes in regular use;

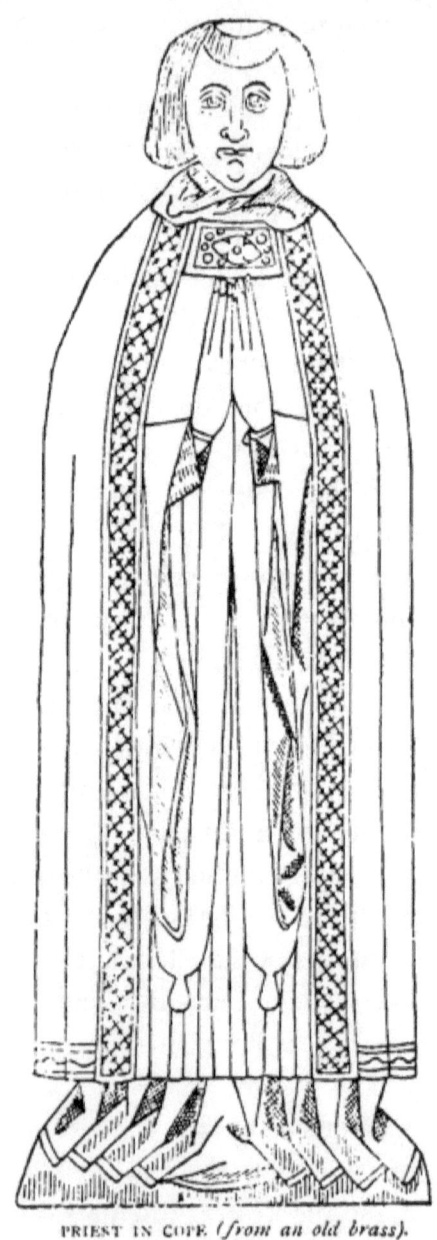

PRIEST IN COPE. *(from an old brass).*

and Exeter, in 1327, had seventy-four. Several of these

were of cloth of gold, others were embroidered all over with flowing patterns, or with designs illustrating some passage of Scripture or the life of a saint. One at Sarum had a silver morse, and was set with fifty-seven small stones, having also on the hood nine more. Several copes had small bells fastened round the edge; Conrad, Abbot of Canterbury, gave to that Cathedral, in 1108, a magnificent cope, embroidered with gold, and having a fringe of one hundred and forty silver bells; another, which belonged to Lanfranc, had fifty-one silver-gilt bells. This obviously was in imitation of the golden bells on the tunic of the Jewish high-priest, but in thus suggesting the comparison, it is strange that they were not put on the sacerdotal chasuble instead of on the cope.

By the time of the Reformation a still more extraordinary number of copes had accumulated in the wealthier churches, most of which were shamelessly stolen by Royal Commission and put to secular and even base purposes. In the days of Edward VI. two hundred and fifty copes, many of them of great splendour, were to be found in S. Paul's alone. In some few cases they were saved from desecration by being cut up to make altar-cloths, or pulpit hangings. But Dr. William Fulke, Master of Pembroke Hall, Cambridge, in a polemical work published in 1580, admits that some had "their beds garnished with old copes," and apparently sees nothing in the sacrilege of which to be ashamed.

Our ecclesiastical monuments and brasses give us many examples of the mediæval copes. The one which illustrates this chapter is from a brass in the Parish Church of Eccleston, near Chorley, in Lancashire. The name of the priest represented is unknown, as the inscription has been destroyed; but it may be assumed that the figure is that of a Vicar of Eccleston. The date of the brass is put at about 1480. The priest is vested as for a solemn procession, in amice, surplice, and cope, all worn over the cassock. The cope is adorned with embroidery round the bottom, and with narrow orphreys down the front: it is clasped with a morse, which is apparently jewelled.

Of the more ornate vestments of the Church, the cope was the most largely retained in use after the disruption of the Reformation period. In 1573, Master Edward Dering asks "How can I subscribe to the ceremonies of Cathedral Churches where they have the priest, deacon, and subdeacon in copes and vestments all as before?" Again, in 1605, the Puritans issued "Certain Demands," one of which was for the abolition of copes, together with surplices, crosses, and other things of ecclesiastical use. Yet two years later Dr. Sparke asserts that he knows of no one who refuses to conform to the twenty-fourth canon, then newly promulgated, which orders that "in all Cathedral and Collegiate Churches the Holy Communion shall be administered upon principal feast-days . . . the principal minister using a decent cope, and being assisted with the gospeller and epistler." At the dedication of the altar of the Collegiate Church at Wolverhampton, on October 10th, 1636, the officiating clergy wore copes. Several of these vestments once belonging to Archbishop Laud, who came to the Primacy in 1633, are still preserved at S. John's College, Oxford; and Cosin, Bishop of Durham from 1660 to 1674, is recorded to have worn one of white satin. The Cathedral of Durham and the Abbey at Westminster preserved the use of the cope longer than any other churches in England. In 1737, Dr. Collis, in his "Rubric of the Church of England Examined," states that "no copes are worn at present in any Cathedral or Collegiate Churches in the ministration of the Holy Communion except in the Churches of Westminster and Durham." Evidence of a similar nature is given by Daniel De Foe in 1762. At last, in the growing carelessness of the English clergy as to all externals, which showed itself in so many ways in the eighteenth and early nineteenth centuries, even Durham discarded its copes, and Westminster alone saw their use, and that only at such state functions as coronations and, occasionally, at funerals of special solemnity.

Palmer, in his "Origines Liturgicæ," says that in accordance with the old English ritual, both bishops and priests might, if they chose, offer the Holy Sacrifice in copes, instead of in chasubles; and such a custom obtains amongst the Armenian and Nestorian Christians of Chaldæa and India. The rubrical direction in the first Prayer Book (1549) of King Edward VI. enjoins the priest at the Eucharist to wear "a white albe plain with a vestment or cope." The second Prayer Book (1552) of that reign distinctly forbids the use of any one of the three. The Injunctions of Queen Elizabeth, issued in 1564, prescribed the cope, and, as we have seen, the canons of 1604 take the same line. The present Ornaments Rubric, which faces the Office for Mattins in our Prayer Book, was inserted in 1559, and was professedly temporary in character, intended to be in force only until "other order shall be taken by the Queen's Majesty, with the advice of her Commissioners;" but seeing that the book has been more than once since then revised, and that the rubric has been retained,—in one instance at any rate (namely in 1662) not by an oversight, but in spite of Puritan opposition,—it seems obvious that the law of the Church at present is that of the Prayer Book of 1549.

The use of gowns, both in church and out, is a matter somewhat analogous to the one that we have been considering; for like the cope, the gown was a habit at one time generally worn by the clergy out of doors, and then by a certain section of them came to be greatly favoured for use during divine service. The gown was originally an adaptation of the monastic habit, which the preaching friars sometimes wore instead of an alb or other recognized ecclesiastical dress. It was of ample width, and had wide sleeves, after the fashion of the more flowing types of gown still worn at English universities, and from its use at those seats of learning was known as the scholar's gown.

At the time of the Reformation it became the accepted dress of the clergy, although the more extreme Puritans protested against it. Archbishop Grindal, writing about the year 1571 to Jerome Zanchy, tells him, almost apologetically, that in England "Ministers are required to wear commonly a long gown, a square cap, and a kind of tippet over the neck, hanging from either shoulder, and falling down almost to their heels." Sandys, Grindal's successor in the See of London, on the latter's translation to York, amongst other injunctions to his clergy, bids them "to observe the appointed apparel; that is, to wear the square cap, the scholar's gown, etc." Harding, Jewel's antagonist, alludes to the practice of wearing "side gowns having large sleeves, with tippets," but refers sarcastically to the extreme men, as "some of more perfection," who donned "Turkey gowns, gaberdines, frocks or night-gowns, of the most lay fashion, for avoiding of superstition." A man of this kind, apparently, was Thomas Cartwright, whom Whitgift reproves for wearing a "Turkey gown and a hat," a practice which marked "such persons as mislike the gown and the square cap, and pretend preciseness about the rest."

The gown continued, however, to be used as the recognized garb of the English clergy down to the time of George II. Several causes, indeed, combined to make it almost an ecclesiastical vestment. The vanity of some of the more wealthy clergy, who appeared in every day life in silken gowns, and especially the introduction of "lectures" or discourses not contemplated by any rubrics of the Prayer Book, led to the introduction of the gown into the use of the Church. Church order prevented its appearance at the Holy Eucharist, or at any recognized office, but it became in the end of the eighteenth century the ordinary garb of the preacher. The Geneva gown, the foreign and Protestant origin of which is sufficiently indicated by its name, had narrower sleeves than that provided by the English academical costume, and was sometimes called a lawyer's gown.

How general the use of one or other of these forms of black gown for the preacher's use had become is illustrated by an article in the *Quarterly Review* of May, 1843, in which the writer seeks to prove that the use of the surplice in the pulpit is "wholly unsanctioned, is forbidden by ecclesiastical authority, is an innovation on the practice of the Church, and contrary to the true reason and distinction on which the varieties of ecclesiastical dress were instituted."

Fortunately this use of the gown is now almost entirely extinct; and to us, to whom the wearing of the surplice by the preacher has become as usual as it is natural and seemly, it is well nigh impossible to realize the heat of controversy which, within the last half century, has raged around such use; or to imagine that a bishop should find it needful to

THE PREACHER'S GOWN AND BANDS.

devote no small portion of a charge to his clergy to the question whether a preacher might, or might not, wear a surplice in the pulpit. Such is the case with a learned charge delivered in 1842 by Dr. Mant, Bishop of Down and

Connor, and of Dromore, who sums up distinctly in favour of the surplice. A legal decision, quite recently given, pronounced the gown a lawful robe for the preacher, the main point in its favour being the plea of long usage. Nevertheless, there appears to be absolutely no authority for its use during the sermon in the course of the Eucharistic office. No other sermons are provided for, as part of the parochial services, in the Prayer Book; all others may be looked on, therefore, rather in the light of lectures or orations, not forming an integral portion of any office. At such times a monk preaches simply in his monastic habit, of which the cassock and gown may be considered the equivalent dress among English secular priests. On this, as on other ecclesiastical matters, however, legal decisions would perhaps exert more influence, if they were not invariably in such things contradictory one of another.

As regards the clergy when not actually officiating, the academical gown has to some extent retained its position to the present day as the "full dress" of the English clergy. When the diocese, or the archdeaconry, is summoned to meet its bishop, or its archdeacon, through the representation of the clergy and the churchwardens, it is still considered that the gown is the correct dress for the former, although even in this respect its use is not so general as was even recently the case. Judged, however, by that most conservative of standards, the etiquette of the Court, a cassock and an academical gown still form the full official dress of the English clergy for secular use.

The only vestment, if so it may be called, which is tolerated by any of the Protestant Nonconformist sects, is the black gown. In individual cases Presbyterian and

Congregationalist ministers wear it while conducting service, with the hood of their degree if they be graduates. There is no general rule, however, and the practice depends on the fancy of the different congregations, or of the preachers. The Moderators of the three Presbyterian bodies in Scotland have an official costume, which has been fixed by continuous usage. The head of the Established Church, or Kirk, wears court dress and an ample gown with full sleeves; the Moderator of the Free Kirk dresses very similarly; while he of the United Presbyterian Kirk uses a Genevan gown and bands.

The cloak or cope in use in the Eastern Church is the *mandyas*, or, in the later form of the word, *mandion*. Its shape was originally similar to that of the Roman *paenula*, though the word is sometimes used of a shorter garment. S. Germanus, appointed Patriarch of Constantinople in the year 715, speaks of this cape or cope as being symbolical, from being "open and simple," of the "winged speed of the angels." It was also thought to mystically commemorate the crimson robe of scorn thrown round the shoulders of our Saviour by the soldiers.

CHAPTER IV.

Head Gear.

THE earliest form of head covering used by the Christian clergy was apparently the cowl, or hood, which formed part of the cloak; the casula and paenula being alike in having this, as in other respects. There was no cap or covering for the head used during the divine offices. In fact, down to the thirteenth century, the ordinary clergy were strictly forbidden to wear anything of the kind in church. Innocent IV., who was made pope in 1243, is said to have been the first to allow any divergence from this rule, when, as a special privilege, he allowed the monks of Canterbury to wear their almuces while saying their offices.

This almuce, or amess (not to be confused with the amice, to be mentioned in a later chapter) was a tippet and hood, lined with fur. Those of the inferior clergy and the monks were lined with dark-coloured furs, and were sometimes called calabres, from the fact that this material was imported from Calabria. A more costly kind was lined with silver-grey fur, and was used by higher dignitaries. Both are mentioned in the "Chronicle of the Grey Friars of London." Under the year 1547 and "the iij. day of June," we are told that "all the gray ammesse, with the calobre in Powlles (S. Paul's Cathedral) were put down." It is from the use of this hood that Milton borrows his figure of "Morning fair," which comes "with pilgrim steps in amice gray." In confirming the privileges of the minor canons of S. Paul's in 1378, Pope Urban VI., in conjunction with the Archbishop of Canterbury, orders that in choir they are to wear white surplices and almuces of black stuff, lined with the skins of various small animals (*de variis minutis*).

The almuce was originally worn as much by laymen as by "clerks." The former, however, discarded its use, and thus, by that conservatism in dress to which allusion has more than once been made, that became distinctively an ecclesiastical dress, which in its origin and nature was not specially connected with the Church.

That something of the kind was necessary for the regular clergy can easily be imagined, especially during their night offices, and for the older members of the community. It must be remembered that nothing was then done to warm the churches, and that the windows were not in all cases even filled with glass. The windows of Peterborough Cathedral were only blocked up with reeds and straw as late as the thirteenth century, and in many places, at a much later date, wooden shutters were the sole protection in the clerestory windows against the wind, rain, or snow. There must have been ample excuse, therefore, for the adoption of a fur tippet and hood when summoned to lauds or prime on a winter's night in the great Cathedral of Canterbury, or any other huge abbey church.

The almuce, like almost everything which even in the remotest way concerned the Church, was dragged into the controversies of the Reformation period. Thomas Cartwright, the Puritan, is chided for his perversity by Archbishop Whitgift, in that while he saw popery and superstition in every vestment which was retained in use, he maintained that the "grey amice" was "a garment of dignity." Its use was forbidden by the bishops in the reign of Elizabeth, on the ground that it was entirely unauthorized.

This tippet, the name of which is variously spelt by the mediæval and reformation writers, as almuce, aumuce, amess, and in yet other ways, was sometimes made with ends hanging over the shoulders in front, something like a modern scarf, though much shorter. A well-known portrait of Archbishop Warham, the immediate predecessor of Thomas Cranmer in the See of Canterbury, shows him wearing such an almuce. Sometimes the tails of the animals, whose skins lined the cape, formed a kind of fringe to it, as in a mediæval miniature of a precentor of Sarum, preserved in the Book of Life of S. Alban's. The "collar of sables" which contemporary records tell us Parker wore at his consecration was an almuce.

A good representation of a mediæval almuce is supplied by a brass in Manchester Cathedral

JOHN HUNTINGDON (*from a brass in Manchester Cathedral*).

to the memory of John Huntington, the first warden of the collegiate body, a post to which he was appointed in 1422, and which he vacated by death in 1458. His effigy is robed as for the usual choir offices, in cassock, surplice, and almuce. The last is decorated with a fringe of tails, and the hood, though turned back, is clearly indicated. In another representation of this garment, also from an old brass, a clasp is seen for fastening it just below the neck, and it terminates in front in two long broad ends.

ALMUCE (*from a brass*).

In the course of time this garment has taken several developments. The hood gave way to the square cap, of which we shall speak presently, and the tippet took various forms in different circumstances. From it arose, according to some, the short cape worn by ecclesiastics of certain ranks in foreign churches; in French cathedrals it has become an ornament of fur, no longer actually worn, but carried over the left arm by the canons. In England its most striking and best known modern form is the academical hood, by which the wearers are distinguished according to the university degrees which they have taken.

The usual colour of an English canon's almuce was black, but the hue varied in different places. Violet was worn at Messina and other churches in Italy, and black, edged with violet, at Palermo. Purple, with a hood of lamb's wool, was the rule at Languedoc; while at Syracuse, at Vienne, and at a few other places the colour varied with the season. The way was therefore already prepared for the many-hued tippets of the modern universities. Doctors of Divinity were permitted to use scarlet almuces, and the colour has survived to this day in their academical hoods, while the ordinary black almuce with its fur lining has not been greatly changed in becoming the hood of the bachelor of arts. Other colours for the other degrees have been adopted by the different universities of Christendom for local or other reasons, which it would be beside our question to enter upon here.

The hood is not an ecclesiastical vestment, but merely part of the academical robes; it has, nevertheless, been given a quasi-ecclesiastical character in England by the fifty-eighth canon, which orders that all "such ministers as are graduates shall wear upon their surplices . . . such hoods as by the orders of the Universities are agreeable to their degrees, which no minister shall wear (being no graduate) under pain of suspension. Notwithstanding it shall be lawful for such ministers as are not graduates to wear upon their surplices, instead of hoods, some decent tippet of black, so it be not silk." The first Prayer Book of Edward VI. was not so absolute in its ruling, and the connection between the use of almuces and that of hoods is certainly suggested by the fact that it is only "in Cathedral Churches and Colleges," that is in churches for the most part formerly monastic, that permission is given to the clergy to "use in quire" the hoods of their degree. It is also suggested as "seemly, that graduates when they preach," should use their hoods. It seems that in pre-reformation times the clergy had adopted the academical hood as part of their secular costume, and that the custom continued, for Perceval Wiburn, writing to the Zurich Protestants an account of the English Church in the reign of Queen Elizabeth, says—"In their external dress the ministers of the word are at this time obliged to conform themselves to that of the popish priests; the square cap is imposed upon all, together with a gown as long and loose as conveniently may be, and to some also is added a silk hood."

Mention is here again made of the clerical use of the square cap, which became, and for a long time remained, the recognized form of sacerdotal head-gear. This began to come into vogue in the sixteenth century, and is mentioned in the proceedings of a synod at Tours, in 1583. An example of its early shape is given us in the accompanying portrait of John Wyclif, taken from Bale's "Centuries of British Writers," published in 1548. It is a stuff cap, sufficiently full to allow of its forming four distinct corners at the top, while behind it comes down over the ears and the back of the head. The cap in which Wolsey is usually depicted is very slightly different; and Holbein's portrait of Cardinal Fisher (now in S. John's College, Cambridge) represents him in a hat of a similar shape.

Great confusion and diversity of dress arose in consequence of the Reformation, which makes Harding demand of Jewel, Bishop of Salisbury, "Among your ministering clergy is not likewise diversity found? Do not some among you wear square caps, some round caps, some button caps, some only hats." This want of uniformity was not pleasing to the powers either of church or state, and Elizabeth accordingly issued that Injunction quoted in a former chapter, prescribing, among other things, the wearing of the square cap; and the bishops proceeded to enforce obedience. Archbishop Parker writes to Sir William Cecil, on the 30th April, 1565, informing him that he had had an interview with two of the London clergy, Sampson and Humphrey by name, and had warned them that they must conform in the matter of the cap and gown, the surplice and the hood, or be deprived of their offices. Sandys, too, shortly after his translation from the See of Worcester to that of London, issued injunctions to the clergy of his new diocese, in one of which, as we saw before, he insists on the square cap. Pilkington, Bishop of Durham, writes to the Earl of Leicester on October 25th, 1564, on behalf of the "refusers of the habits;" "There is great offence taken," he says, "with some of the ministry for not using such apparel as the rest do;" and he goes on later to point out that "Bucer, when he was asked why he did not wear the square cap (quadrato pileo), made answer, 'Quia caput non est quadratum.'" Grindal, Hooper, Whitgift, and other writers of the period refer to the question; and in fact an absurd amount of trouble seems to have been taken to enforce the use, and an

JOHN WYCLIF *(Bales Centuries of British Writers, 1548).*

unaccountable amount of heat shown in opposition to it, when we consider the carelessness with which points of ritual of infinitely greater moment were abandoned, or allowed to lapse into disuse. So bitter was the dislike to the square cap felt by Turner, Dean of Wells, that in 1565 he made a common adulterer do penance wearing a cap of that kind. To such an unseemly pitch did he suffer his passion to lead him.

The gradual development of the square cap of the sixteenth century into the college cap of the nineteenth is easily seen if one has an opportunity of comparing the portraits of a series of ecclesiastics of the first-named and of the following century. We see first of all the cap such as it is portrayed in the portraits above referred to of Wyclif, Wolsey, and Fisher. The top of this cap grows wider as years go by, generally keeping the square form with the corners at the front, back, and sides of the head; although some were made round, very like the cap now called "a Tam o' Shanter," a shape which has become associated with the name of Bishop Andrewes, whose episcopate, first at Chichester, and then at Ely and at Winchester, lasted from 1605 to 1625. At

CARDINAL WOLSEY.

last we find that the hat has become just like that now worn by collegians, except that the square top is stiffened only by the double thickness of the stuff itself, and the lower part, of the same material, curves out into the flat part above. From this it was but a little step, and one calculated to make the hat lighter for wearing, to make the top of thinner stuff stiffened out with cardboard, and to attach it to a skull cap beneath.

On the Continent, however, these later phases of development in the square cap have not taken place, and among us the old form, or at any rate a much nearer approach to it than the college cap supplies, has recently been revived from foreign sources, as is implied by its Italian name of biretta. In a former chapter allusion was made to the short cloak which, under the name of the birrus, was in early times commonly worn by all classes of the people. The hood which was attached to this has given us the biretta, just as the hood of the almuce became the old English square cap. The cloak in question was generally made of ruddy woollen material, or of a tawny fur; hence, according to some authorities, the name is derived from *pyrrhus*, or *purros*, meaning flame-coloured. A biretta is seen on the head of the Augustinian Canon engraved in a former chapter.

In the East the popes, or parish priests, wear a circular, brimless hat. Deacons and sub-deacons in the Armenian Church wear a cylindrical cap, ornamented with embroidery, and their priests a kind of crown surmounted by a cross.

From some such original as this last-named ornament the episcopal mitre has grown. Eusebius calls it a crown (*stephanos*), and S. Gregory Nazianzen a diadem (*kidaris*), and, in fact, "crown" became almost a synonym for the episcopate. Thus in addresses of respect it was usual to appeal to the bishop for attention and regard "*per coronam*." S. Augustine, writing at the end of the fourth century to Proculeianus, a Donatist bishop, reminds him of their mutual relations in the words,—"Your people honour us, and ours honour you; yours appeal to us by our crown, and by your crown ours appeal to you." Some have sought to

CARDINAL JOHN FISHER *(From Portrait by Holbein).*

show that the tonsure, which certainly was often spoken of as a crown, is all that is here referred to; and others, as Bingham in his "Antiquities of the Christian Church," have held that the expression is purely metaphorical. The commonness of the phrase seems, however, to imply the use of some material crown which gave rise to it; and the limitation of the word to the episcopate, points to the fact that such an ornament was part of the exclusive insignia of a bishop, whereas the tonsure was worn also by the other clerical orders.

The earliest mitres were simply bands or fillets of linen; and even in this primitive form, they were probably not worn universally by bishops, nor even reckoned as part of the usual episcopal costume until a comparatively late date. Walafrid Strabo, Abbot of Rosenau, near Constance, in the middle of the ninth century, writes concerning "Holy Vessels and Vestments;" yet he makes no mention of the mitre. Nevertheless John of Cappadocia, Bishop of Contantinople in the sixth century, wore a circlet, which he was the first to adorn with gold and with sacred figures painted or embroidered on it. Not before the year 1000 A.D., however, can we reckon the mitre as part of the recognized episcopal habit. It is rather curious that at the present day the patriarchate of Constantinople is one of the few districts where mitres are quite unknown, the bishops celebrating the divine offices uncovered at all times, while in their secular dress they wear only a kind of loose hood. The Russian and Armenian bishops use an official head-gear very similar to the most primitive mitres, namely a coronet or diadem.

In the West the episcopal crown, once fairly introduced, grew in height and in splendour. One of the earliest, if not quite the first, existing representation of one is in the Benedictional of S. Ethelwald (now in the library of the Duke of Devonshire), which probably dates from the tenth century, where one of the bishops is figured wearing about his brows a gold circlet set with gems. The first undoubted mention of a mitre is in the following century, when we find, among other instances, a charter of Leo X., granted to Archbishop Eberhard, of Trèves, in which the Pope allows the Archbishop and his successors the use of "a Roman mitre." Peter Damian also at the end of that century, writing to the antipope, suggests that the latter has probably assumed "the mitre and the red cope according to the custom of the Roman pontiff."

From these expressions it would appear that the use of the mitre was not at first considered an episcopal right, but that, in Western Christendom at any rate, it began at Rome, and was granted to favoured sees by the Pope; until, the grant having become very general, it came to be regarded as a prerogative of all prelates. The See of Hamburgh claims that the privilege was granted to its bishops by Leo IV. (847), and Utrecht traces the use to a decree of Alexander III. (1159).

The earliest change in the form of the crown was produced by raising the sides, allowing it to be hollowed out crescent-wise in front and back. When it became a cap rather than a crown it was made of linen, but by the thirteenth century it had become more costly in material and adornment, for Durandus refers to the linen mitre as being in accordance with "the former custom." A manuscript of the eleventh century in the British Museum represents S. Dunstan fully vested and enthroned; he wears a round, low cap, with short *infulæ*, or ribbons, falling behind. Two centuries later it had attained practically the shape now in use, save that it was of small dimensions, standing only some six or eight inches above the forehead. Mitres, up to the fourteenth century, preserved a graceful outline, and reasonable proportions, but after that they grew in height and breadth, until in most continental examples they appear ponderous and inartistic.

They were originally provided with two ribbons, or fanons, which were tied beneath the chin to secure the mitre in place; these have now become merely ornamental pendants, falling over the bishop's shoulders.

MITRE OF S. THOMAS A BECKET.

That even in mediæval times there were, nevertheless, considerable differences in the size and shape of the mitres, the illustrations in various parts of this book will clearly show. The mitre of S. Thomas à Becket, martyred in 1170, which is now preserved at Sens, and the splendid Limerick mitre, which dates from 1408, illustrate two extremes; the first being low and but bluntly pointed, the other running to a sharp point at a considerable height. In each case, however, the outline consists of straight lines, the curved examples being much later in date.

Robert Pursglove, bishop suffragan of Hull in the days of Queen Mary, whose figure from a brass at Tideswell, in Derbyshire, will be found on a subsequent page, is represented as wearing a mitre of very similar proportions to that of S. Thomas. On the other hand, a brass at Manchester with the effigy of James Stanley, Bishop of Ely, and a successor of Huntington in the wardenship of the college at Manchester, shows him with a mitre more considerable in height, the sides of which are slightly curved. Each of these mitres is of the type known as a precious mitre, from being adorned with embroidered orpheys and jewels, and made of some handsome material. For penitential seasons and the lesser functions in which the bishop takes part, the simple mitre is provided.

Pope Alexander II. (1061) granted to the Abbot of S. Augustine's Abbey at Canterbury the privilege of wearing the mitre. This was not the earliest instance of its non-episcopal use, for Leo IX. (1049) had already conferred upon the Canons of Bamberg the unusual honour of officiating in mitres. It was, however, the commencement of what became practically a right vested in the rulers of the more important monastic houses. Westminster

LIMERICK MITRE.

Abbey was granted the mitre in 1167; Waltham in 1191; Thorney in 1200; and at various dates carrying us down to the fifteenth century all the wealthier abbeys of England followed. The Prior of Durham received the mitre in 1374, and in 1386 the Prior of Winchester. This non-episcopal use of episcopal insignia was not, however, altogether approved of in England. It formed one of the points of suggested reformation in the Church, named in articles presented to King Henry V. in 1414 with that intent by the University of Oxford.

The first mitred abbot in France was Hugh of Clugny, to whom permission to assume it was given by Urban II., himself a Frenchman, in 1088, S. Denys, Monte Cassino, Vendôme, and other places subsequently had the same privilege given them; in fact the use of the mitre grew so common among the heads of monastic houses, that it became needful to make distinctions amongst the wearers. Pope Clement IV. (1265) ordered that only exempt abbots (the rulers of abbeys acknowledging no "visitor" except the pope) might wear the "precious mitre," while others were to employ a plain one. In the case of abbots of inferior abbeys the mitre properly has no indentation. This ecclesiastical crown, although strictly part of the episcopal insignia, has been in several other instances granted to ecclesiastics as an unusual and peculiar privilege. The Dean, the Chancellor, the Treasurer, and the Archdeacon of Toledo have enjoyed this distinction since 1317; the Dean, the Provost, and the Chanter of Mayence have the same special dignity; as have also the Provosts of Vienne, Macon, Ghent, S. Die, and Lavantz. The celebrant at Cambrai, and the celebrant, deacon, and subdeacon at Vienne and Macon, also had this privilege allowed them. The canons, not only of Bamberg, as mentioned above, but also of Lisbon, Pisa, Besançon, Puy, Rodez, Brionde, Solsona, Messina, Salerno, Naples, Lyons, and Lucca, all enjoyed this special distinction.

In England the mitred abbots came of necessity to an end with the dissolution and destruction of their abbeys. The mitre gradually died out of use among the bishops in the general discarding of external marks of dignity and splendour which followed the Reformation; but there are sufficient instances of its appearance at irregular intervals for us to be able to claim that in theory at least it never was entirely abandoned.

William Tyndale, in his "Obedience of a Christian Man," published in 1528, counts mitres, along with rochets, crosiers, and other episcopal insignia, among the "false signs" of antichrist. And so early as 1561, Pilkington, Bishop of Durham, had so far departed from the stateliness formerly found especially in that princely see, that he declares he has "neither cruche (crosier) nor mitre." Yet mitres and crosiers of silver gilt were carried at the funerals of Duppa, Bishop of Winchester, in 1662, Archbishop Juxon, of Canterbury, in 1663, Archbishop Frewen, of York, in 1664, Cosin, Bishop of Durham, in 1674, and Trelawny, Bishop of Bristol, in 1721. The mitre alone was used at the funerals of bishops of Bristol and elsewhere within the present century. The bishops wore mitres at the coronation of George III. The first bishops of the Anglican Communion in the United States of America assumed the mitre, and two of the earliest examples used by them are still preserved. In quite recent years the English episcopate has in several instances turned what had become a merely heraldic use of the mitre in connection with their shields of arms, or the tombs of prelates, into a reality, by once more adopting this ancient and dignified emblem of apostolic authority.

In the seventeenth century the custom arose of depicting the mitres of the English archbishops encircled by a marquis's coronet; and still later by that of a duke. This is supposed to represent the temporal as well as the ecclesiastical rank of the occupants of the primatial sees; but, as a matter of fact, such a representation is a modern device of heralds only, devoid of any ancient authority. The Bishop of Durham, however, who until 1833 was, in virtue of his episcopal rank, also prince palatine of the north, had a right to the use of a coronet.

The broad-brimmed scarlet hat of the cardinals was granted them by Pope Paul II. (1464-1471), having been formerly a form of head-gear distinctively papal. Innocent IV., more than two hundred years before, had allowed them the use of red caps, similar to those at that time worn by legates *à latere*. The scarlet knots with which the strings of the hat are fringed were originally three in number, but were afterwards increased to five. Christ Church College, Oxford, founded by Cardinal Wolsey under the name of Cardinal College in the year 1526, still carries the cardinal's hat as a crest above its coat-of-arms. The arms of Bishop Sherborn, who held the See of Chichester from 1508 to 1536, are represented in his cathedral surmounted by a cardinal's hat instead of a mitre, although he was a bishop merely.

The tiara worn by the Roman Pontiff was adorned with two crowns by Boniface VIII. (1299-1303) to render it symbolical of the temporal as well as the spiritual jurisdiction which he claimed. The third crown was added by Urban V. (1362-1370). A manuscript written by Matthew Paris about 1250, and now in the British Museum, has an illustration representing Pope Adrian I. receiving a letter from Offa II. of Mercia. The Pope wears a conical hat surmounted by a cross, and having a single crown encircling it. Some bishops, it is alleged, before the introduction of mitres, wore a pointed hat of this kind under the name of *phrygium*, presumably from its likeness to that cap which, as the Phrygian cap, afterwards became a badge of popular liberty. Archbishop Jewel quotes John of Paris (who flourished about 1290) as saying that Pope S. Sylvester had a phrygium composed of peacock's feathers. The modern papal *regnum*, as the tiara is more accurately called, is formed by the addition of three crowns to a hat of this ancient form.

Josephus tells us that the Jewish High Priest had upon his cap or mitre "a circlet of gold wrought in three tiers," which may have been in allusion to his combined judicial and sacerdotal authority.

In concluding this chapter a word or two on the clerical tonsure will not be out of place; for although the fashion of cutting and wearing the hair scarcely forms part of the dress, it certainly has its influence upon it. In the next chapter we shall see that the use of wigs by the English clergy in the eighteenth century probably affected the shape of the surplice; and similarly there can be little question that the use of the tonsure by monks and ecclesiastics had much to do with the introduction of the various head-coverings for use in church.

The feeling in which the tonsure originated is very

ancient. Among the Jews the custom was known as an expression of overwhelming sorrow. "They shall not be buried," exclaims the prophet Jeremiah, "neither shall men lament for them, nor cut themselves, nor make themselves bald for them." And again, Micah cries to the people, "Make thee bald and poll thee for thy delicate children, enlarge thy baldness as the eagle, for they are gone into captivity from thee." The practice of shaving the head in the Christian Church arose from a similar feeling—that of sorrow for the sins of the world, or of penitence for one's own. Penitents were shorn as part of their penance, as appears from Paulinus and the third Council of Toledo (589 A.D.), and for this reason it was held by S. Jerome and others that such a practice was unbecoming the clergy.

The ecclesiastics of the first centuries, however, wore their hair and beards clipt short, as was the mode in imperial Rome; and just as their conservative adherence to the old garb of the city marked them off from others after the barbarian invasion, so when those same barbarians introduced the fashion of long hair and flowing beards, the same clinging to older ways was a further mark of distinction with the Christian priesthood.

The circular tonsure does not appear to have originated in Rome. Some of the earliest allusions to it, dating as far back as the sixth century, refer to Gaul, S. Gregory of Tours (died 594) having the first undoubted reference to it. From about this time the use of the coronal tonsure spread in Western Christendom, and many councils and provincial synods passed decrees enforcing it. In England there seems to have been a constantly recurring tendency to escape the rule if possible. In 950 it was ordered in

Northumbria, that a priest who did not shave his beard and his hair, or who concealed his tonsure, should be fined. The Council of Westminster, in 1173, forbade the presentation of any clerk who had not "the mark of clerical distinction" to a benefice; and a council at York, in 1195, ordered in the case of beneficed priests who had not the tonsure, the alternative of their deprivation or their shaving "against their will by the archdeacon or the dean." The Constitutions of Archbishop Boniface, given at Lambeth in 1261, again refer to the subject, and give at the same time the mystical meaning at that time assigned to the tonsure. It is commanded, "That bishops in synod, archdeacons and deans in chapter, and chaplains in church, proclaim thrice yearly that all who wish to enjoy the clerical privilege are to have a decent tonsure and a shaven crown, and let them not be ashamed to bear the marks of Him, who deigned for their sakes to wear a crown of thorns." Councils at Exeter in 1287, at London in 1342, and others, all speak to the same effect.

The old British tonsure, known as the tonsure of S. John, consisted in the shaving of the fore-part of the head in a semi-circle. The Roman tonsure, or that of S. Peter, is in the form of a complete circle on the top of the head, and the difference between the two formed one of the points of argument between the British Church and S. Augustine and his followers. The tonsure of S. Paul, at one time observed in the East, consisted in cropping the whole head as short as possible. Strictly, the Roman tonsure should always consist of the ample circle seen on the head of the monks, but since the eleventh century it has been gradually contracted by priests working in the world to a very small size.

The full tonsure of the Middle Ages is illustrated by the figures of Huntington and the priest in a cope, already given; and still better by that of Edmund Assheton on a later page.

Doubtless, as intimated above, the use of head-coverings in church, beginning as it did with concessions to monastic communities, was allowed as a protection to tonsured heads against cold, especially during the night offices.

CHAPTER V.

Linen and Lawn.

WE have already seen that in the primitive Church the clothing of the clergy, especially the garments worn in their public ministrations, consisted largely of white linen. The tradition of this use is still marked in the vestments of the Christian ministry, some linen robes, even when supplemented with others of silk or other more costly fabrics, being used in all the Church's offices, and by all her officers.

Of all the vestments used in the church the alb has probably kept the nearest to its primitive make in shape, colour, and material. The simple linen tunic, reaching sometimes to the the feet, and fitted with sleeves, was, as we have seen, a common garment with all classes in the first century. There is evidence to show that even as late as the ninth century it was worn by laymen in some parts of Germany, but long before that it had come to be considered over the greater part of Christendom as an exclusively clerical dress, and had already assumed its present name of *alb*. A glance at the alb here engraved, and at the fresco from the

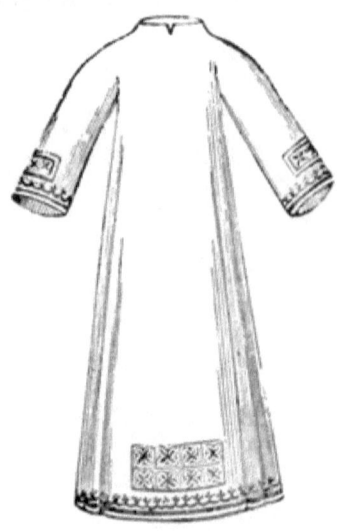

ALB *(Pugin's Ecclesiastical Costume)*.

Catacomb in the first chapter, will at once show how nearly this vestment resembles the primitive dress.

The canons of the fourth Council of Carthage, A.D. 398, allude to the use of albs by deacons, and, although doubt has been thrown on the authenticity of this Council, its alleged canons are admitted to be of about the date named. The alb is also referred to by the Council of Narbonne in 589, and in the canons of Ælfric in 957. The name, it is scarcely needful to point out, was derived from its earliest, and its constantly most usual, colour. Other names were given to it, however, in early times, such as *camisia, poderis, linea*, and others. Isidore, writing in 595, says—"The poderis is a linen tunic worn by priests, fitting closely to the body and coming down to the feet; this is commonly called camisia." The corresponding vestment in the East is the *stoicharion*.

The councils, above referred to, prove in their canons that the alb was from the first one of the garments worn at the Holy Eucharist; being originally the characteristic vestment of the deacon and subdeacon, but worn also by the priest, as now, beneath the outer and more flowing robe which has become the modern chasuble.

The names linea and alba would seem to limit the material and the colour of this vestment very distinctly, and as a matter of fact it has remained faithful to the literal meaning of its names to a greater extent than is usually found in the case of things and names of such ancient date. Nevertheless it has not always been made of linen, nor always white in colour. According to William of Malmesbury, Brithwold, an early bishop of Salisbury, had a most precious alb of silk; William de Longchamp gave a silk alb to Ely in 1197;

Richard of London gave an alb of red samite, embroidered in gold, in 1270. In 1295, Canterbury Cathedral possessed 132 albs of silk, and in 1321 it had also others of samite. Bishop Galfrid left by will in 1140 two samite albs; Bishop Beck similarly bequeathed in 1310 albs of cloth of gold. Most of the older inventories of our Cathedrals would supply other illustrations.

As to the colour, great latitude was at one time allowed. Winchelsey, Archbishop of Canterbury (1294-1313), had albs of the liturgical colours, corresponding with the other vestments. Bishop Bartholomew (1161-1185) gave to Exeter Cathedral two albs of blue; and allusions are of frequent occurrence to albs of red samite, and to others of green, indigo, and other hues. At the funeral of Poore, Bishop of Durham, which took place in 1237, a black alb was worn; and there are other instances of albs of this colour.

Coloured albs, and those of other materials than of linen, have gone out of use once more, and the more primitive custom prevails; though such vestments were worn at Angers, and at other places in France so late as 1750. They seem never to have been so common elsewhere as in England; of their use over the greater part of the Continent there is no trace at all.

The mediæval albs were frequently most splendidly adorned with "apparels," or patches of embroidery, on the cuffs, and along the bottom in front and behind. At Salisbury, in 1222, was an alb embroidered with lions; at Peterborough, in 1184, white silk albs with red parures, or apparels; at Exeter, about the same time, an alb embroidered with the figures of archers, and another with moons and stars. We find in inventories of church property during the middle ages numbers of albs embroidered with pearls and jewels, and with elaborate and costly needle-work. An alb of the fourteenth century is preserved in the South Kensington Museum; its apparels are of silk, embroidered in gold, and a narrow stripe of work in white runs across the shoulders with the words "Jesus-Maria" on either side. The alb of S. Thomas of Canterbury is treasured at Sens; it has a bold pattern on a wide apparel in front.

Clergy in England who are anxious to maintain or revive what are supposed to be old English traditions sometimes use albs with embroidered apparels; but as a rule, in those churches where the Eucharistic vestments are found in use, simple linen ones are worn. These are, however, sometimes embroidered in coloured silks, and occasionally deep lace replaces a corresponding depth of linen at the bottom, some handsome albs being entirely lace from the waist downwards.

At the Reformation the alb, despite its undoubted antiquity, came in for its share in the attack which the extreme men levelled at almost every custom which had formerly been in vogue. All vestments to such men were superstitious abominations, and albs among the rest. Archbishop Grindal, in his injunctions to the churchwardens of the diocese of York in 1571, gives a comprehensive list of things, albs among the number, which were not only to be disused, but "utterly defaced, broken, and destroyed;" and should the churchwardens not be able to get hold of all the matters mentioned for this truly Protestant purpose, they were to report those in whose custody the vessel or vestments was, that "further order might be taken for the defacing thereof." Grindal was afterwards translated to Canterbury, and at once started on a similar crusade in the southern province. In 1576 he held, as already pointed out, a "Metropolitical Visitation," in which he made enquires almost identical in terms with those just quoted.

In the first Prayer Book of King Edward VI. (1549) candidates for priests' orders were bidden to present themselves to the bishop vested in "plain albes." The bishop was enjoined when he "celebrated the holy communion in the church, or executed any other public ministration," to wear " beside his rochette, a surplice or albe, and a cope or vestment"; and the priest likewise was to don a "white albe plain with a vestment or cope," when he celebrated "the Holy Communion, commonly called the Mass"; while any others who might assist were to wear "albes with tunicles." Even in saying the "Ante-communion office," which was to follow the Litany every Wednesday and Friday, the priest was ordered to wear "a plain albe or surplice with a cope." All this was altered by the second book in 1552, when one general direction at the commencement of the work orders that "the minister at the time of the communion and at all other times in his ministration shall use neither alb, vestment, nor cope." This again was altered, and we were thrown back apparently, as we have seen in a former chapter, on the earlier order of things by the Ornaments Rubric of the present Prayer Book.

In early times the linen tunic, or alb, fell ungirt to the knees or the feet as the case might be. A writer of the sixth century, calling himself Germanus of Paris, says, "The alb is not confined by a girdle, but hangs down covering the body of the Levite." Later, however, it became customary to wear a zone or girdle with the alb. As this change took place at about the time when Christian writers were dwelling a good deal on the analogy between the vestments of the Old and those of the New Dispensation, it seems not improbable that the girdle was deliberately borrowed from Jewish usage, so as to strengthen that analogy.

The early girdles were belts, fastened with a clasp, and often elaborately ornamented. Riculfus, bishop of Soissons in 915, mentions in his will "five zones," one of which was adorned with gold and precious stones, and the remaining four with gold. Most of our Church inventories take note of the girdles used by the clergy. At Salisbury in 1222 there were twenty-one girdles, nine of them being of silk. One found on the body of S. Cuthbert at Durham was of gold tissue interwoven with scarlet thread, and was nearly an inch wide.

With the disuse of silk albs, silk girdles have also disappeared; a white cord is now its practically invariable form, having a tassel at each end.

Most of the Eastern Churches number a cincture, or girdle, among their recognised vestments; with the Greeks, the Syrian Christians, and the Copts, it holds a similar place to the one which it occupies according to Western usage.

The surplice is simply another form of the alb, a form which it naturally has taken in cases where it is intended for other services than the Eucharist. In such offices another vestment seldom being worn over it, it has been made fuller than the alb, has wider sleeves, and is generally shorter, although the oldest surplices reached to the feet. The name, which implies that it was worn over the habit or cassock of skins (*superpellicium*), is met with as early as the days of S. Edward the Confessor, who in one of his laws, enacted in 1060, speaks of "clerks clad in surplices." An old English name for it, found in the canons of Edgar, is *oferslipe*, or overslip.

It appears from many canons, provincial or otherwise, that the surplice was regarded as the minimum of decency in the way of vestments for all kinds of ministrations. The Council of Oxford (1222), after prescribing at least two sets of sacerdotal vestments for each church, goes on to order that all who minister at the Altar should wear surplices. Archbishop Edmund (1234-1245) of Canterbury bids his clergy wear surplice and stole in visiting the sick, unless the distance to be traversed was very great; a successor in the primacy, John Peckham (1278-1294), directs the same robes to be worn when the priest carries the Blessed Sacrament to any one; and provincial statutes promulgated by Winchelsey of Canterbury (1294-1313), Alexander Neville of York (1374-1388), and others, order the surplice to be worn, even if no other robe be forthcoming, at mattins and vespers, processions and masses, and in other divine offices. The Synod of Winchester (1308), however, ordained that in all benefices of the value of fifty marks and upwards, at least one set of Eucharistic vestments must be provided.

The earliest surplices reached to the feet, at any rate in England and in Belgium; but by degrees they were suffered to be worn much shorter. In 1435 the Council of Basle orders canons of cathedrals to wear surplices that reached below the middle of the leg; the Roman tendency, however, was to shorten them, so that Cardinal Bona tells us, in the beginning of the seventeenth century, that at Rome the surplice "scarcely reached to the knee." The shape and size of the old English surplices are shown in some of the brasses to which reference has already been made. The unknown priest interred at Eccleston is depicted in a surplice of the same length as his cope; it falls in many folds about him, and has wide sleeves reaching well below the knee of the wearer. The surplice of John Huntington, shown in his brass at Manchester, is similar in all respects. These are both examples dating from the latter half of the fifteenth century.

The only form of ornamentation found on the surplice is a trimming of lace, occasionally seen round the sleeves and on the bottom. In the very short surplices now frequently seen in England, and known by the Italian name of cotta, this lace is almost always found; but old engravings prove that neither the shape nor the trimming of these vestments is so modern as many people suppose. A copy of the Book of Common Prayer, published in London in 1684, has an engraving of a priest kneeling before an altar, apparently saying the Litany; he wears a cassock, a cotta trimmed with lace, and a skull-cap. A very similar picture is found in a quaint book published by William Battersby of London, in 1700, being the eighth edition of Sparke's "Scintilla Altaris; Primitive Devotion in the Feasts of the Church of England"; the priest is here vested precisely similarly.

The practice of slitting the surplice open down the front, so as to put it on like a gown, is a corrupt custom found only in the English Church, and arising there only during the last century. It has been suggested that it arose as a consequence of the clergy wearing wigs, over which it was hardly possible to slip the surplice in the proper way. The rise of the habit of preaching in a black gown may also have had something to do with it; the open surplice being more quickly slipt off than the closed one. Pepys, in his diary, under date October 26th, 1662, notices the awkwardness arising from the clergyman's change of his surplice, saying "it seemed absurd for him to pull it over his eares in the reading-pew, after he had done, before all the church, to go up to the pulpitt to preach without it."

The simplicity of the surplice, and its consistent freedom from costliness or brilliancy in adornment, have not saved it from Puritan attack. Peter Martyr, in a letter dated at Zurich, November 4th, 1559, tells us that, when at Oxford, he declined to wear a surplice in the choir; and another letter sent by Lawrence Humphrey to Bullinger, also a German divine, in July 1566, shows the lack of decency and order in which some of the reformers gloried. "In the time of the most serene King Edward the Sixth," the writer says, "the Lord's Supper was celebrated in simplicity in many places without the surplice." Jewel, Bishop of Salisbury, sympathized with these extreme notions, and counted "the linen surplice" amongst "the vestiges of error" which it were well to have removed. Cox, Bishop of Ely, on the other hand, defended its use as a primitive custom. And so the dissention ran, the quarrel being largely kept up by the foreign Protestants of Geneva and their English allies; the frequent correspondence which passed between them being full of allusions to the subject. A natural result of the controversy was the display of actual opposition to the surplice now and again. Sir William Cecil, complaining to Archbishop Parker in 1561 (August 12th) of the state of the diocese of Norwich, says that he is informed that the bishop (Parkhurst) "winketh at schismatics and anabaptists;" and that "a surplice may not be borne here;

and the ministers follow the folly of the people, calling it charity to feed their fond humour." Richard Beaumont, Master of Trinity College, and Vice-Chancellor of Cambridge, reports to the same primate in 1564, that "one in Christ's College, and sundry in St. John's, will be very hardly brought to wear surplices." A couple of years later something like a brawl took place at S Giles's, Cripplegate, on some "singing men" appearing in surplices at a funeral. Crowley, the incumbent, with his curate expelled them from the church, and made so much commotion that a complaint was lodged with Archbishop Parker against them. That prelate sat in judgment on the two clerics on the 4th April, 1566; and finding Crowley disposed to defend his action, and rather anxious to have "the glory to be committed to prison," he sentenced him "to keep his house," and bound over "one Sayer, the alderman's deputy," who had shewn great partiality to the defendants in the brawl, in one hundred pounds to produce both of them when called upon. The spirit of the Puritans is well shown by an extract from the journal of William Dowsing, who in 1643 and 1644 visited the Suffolk churches with full authority to destroy all that was of a superstitious nature. Thus he writes:—"Elmet, Aug. 22: Crow, a deputy, had done before we came. We rent apieces there the hood and surplice."

Hooker devotes a portion of the fifth book of his "Ecclesiastical Polity"—the first editon of which bears date 1594—to answering the Puritan objections to this seemly and simple vesture, and in the course of his argument he quotes some of the ludicrously exaggerated language of his opponents. "Their allegations were," he says, "that this popish apparel, the surplice especially, hath been by Papists abominably abused; that it hath been a mark and a very sacrament of abomination; that remaining, it serveth as a monument of idolatry, and not only edifieth not, but as a dangerous and scandalous ceremony doth exceeding much harm to them of whose good we are commanded to have regard; that it causeth men to perish and make shipwreck of conscience; . . . that it hardeneth Papists, hindereth the weak from profiting in the knowledge of the Gospel, grieveth godly minds, and giveth them occasion to think hardly of their ministers; . . . that by the Law it should have been burnt and consumed with fire as a thing infected with leprosy." All these examples of wild declamation are quoted by Hooker from the writings of the Puritan Cartwright. Such fanatical folly surely carries with it its own refutation.

The question of the use of the surplice was again raised, but without effect, by the Puritans at the Hampton Court Conference, under James I. The Canons Ecclesiastical of 1604 re-affirmed the propriety of such use. On the restoration of Charles II. a last attempt was made in this and other details to retain the Puritan ascendancy of the Commonwealth period. A conference met at the Savoy Palace in 1661, at which the grievances of the Puritans were formulated, the use of the surplice, cope, and other robes prescribed in the canons being one. Once more the attempt to make further alterations in church order proved entirely ineffectual; and since then no formal effort in the same direction has been made.

Yet another development of that same long linen tunic which has given us alb, surplice, and cotta, meets us in the rochet, which was originally simply a surplice less full both in the body and the sleeves than the ordinary ones, and therefore adopted by bishops as more convenient for general wear beneath a cope, than a wider robe would be. Mediæval allusions to its use by other orders of the clergy are not rare. Leofric, Bishop of Exeter (1046-1072), bequeathed to his Cathedral three "pistel roccas," or rochets for the use of epistolers at mass; and a synod held at Liège, in 1287, orders priests, when vesting for mass, to wear beneath their albs "surplices, or the linen tunic commonly called a saroth or rochet." The modern name, which is from the same root as the German *rock* (a coat), did not come into use till about the thirteenth century; the garment, however, under other names, such as sarcos, the white camisia, the rosetta, and others, is far more ancient.

Canon law ordained that the rochet should be the proper dress for a bishop whenever he appeared in public, and such it continued to be in England later than in most other countries. Erasmus was surprised that Bishop Fisher laid aside his rochet when travelling. Archbishop Parker when, with the Bishops of Lincoln and Rochester, he received Queen Elizabeth at Canterbury Cathedral, in March, 1575, says that all three of them were "in chimmers and rochets." This latter instance, however, was scarcely one of an ordinary kind; and as a rule the English bishops do not now wear their rochets out of church except in Convocation and in the House of Lords.

The mediæval rochets are described as having narrow sleeves; it was about the time of Bishop Overall, in the first part of the seventeenth century, that the sleeves began to grow to that grotesque size they afterwards attained. They were till lately almost always fastened to the chimere, and the rochet was sleeveless; probably from the difficulty of passing such monstrous creations through the armhole of the former. More reasonable ideas, however, now prevail; and the rochet often appears with sleeves after the primitive fashion, and seldom, if ever, with them of any great size; they are also really attached in most instances to the garment to which they belong, and not to the chimere.

Some continental canons cut down the rochet to the smallest dimensions. In some places the sleeves were cut entirely away, without being replaced in any similar fashion to those of an English bishop; but in the Abbey of Chancellade and elsewhere the sides were also cut open, so that only a broad piece of linen falling before and behind, somewhat like a monastic scapular, was left. The canons of the congregation of S. Rufus diminished it until only a band of two fingers' breadth remained, which was worn sometimes in front only.

One other linen vestment remains to be considered—the amice—which ritually is more closely allied to the alb than those which have just occupied our attention, although it was natural, for historic reasons, to treat of the alb, surplice, and rochet together.

The amice is a square, or oblong, piece of linen, provided with strings attached to the opposite corners of one of its longer sides; it is the first vestment put on by the priest when preparing to offer the Holy Eucharist, and in its final position forms a kind of collar, the strings being wound about the body and tied in front. This, at least, is the usual custom now in the West; it seems, however, that at one time it was assumed after the alb and girdle. Such was the use at Rome, at Milan, and at Lyons, and probably the general one in the eleventh century. The Maronites wear it thus to the present day; and the Armenians use a kind of amice, called a *vakass*, to which a breast plate is attached, and which is put on over the stoicharion, the oriental alb. Otherwise this vestment is unknown in the East, amongst the Greeks, Syrians, and Copts.

Early names for the amice, which means a "wrap" (from amictus), were anagolagium or anagolagus, a neckerchief, and humeral or superhumeral, from the fact that the lower part covered the shoulders. It was also used as a temporary covering for the head; at S. Maurice, Angers, the sacred ministers at Mass kept it over the head until the singing of the Sanctus, when they turned it back over the chasuble; and in many French churches, before the biretta came into general use, it was customary to go to the altar with the amice over the head. On the Percy tomb in Beverley Minster is the figure of a priest with the amice apparently worn in this manner A relic of this custom remains in the fact that the priest in assuming it rests it upon his head while adjusting it, and then turn or rolls it back, so as to cover the back of the stole. An ancient missal at Narbonne speaks of the amice under the name of *galea*, or helmet, in obvious allusion to this practice; and in the mystical meaning assigned to each of the vestments, this one, for the same reason, is spoken of as "the helmet of salvation."

The amice is the latest of the Eucharistic vestments in coming into use, and is traced to no primitive original. It was indeed, in all probability, simply a prudent precaution to preserve the stole and chasuble from getting soiled by contact with the skin. So long, therefore, as all the sacerdotal robes were of linen, or other simple material, an amice was not needful; but when these came to be made of costly silks and satins, covered with elaborate embroidery, and heavy at times with jewels and the precious metals, it then became necessary to take every care to preserve them. The amice, for this reason, is not reckoned amongst the recognized vestments before the ninth century, although probably it was worn, on simply practical grounds, without ritual authority, before.

In the course of time the special reason of its existence was lost sight of, and at one period it became as ornate in material and decoration as we have seen the alb once was; the two vestments in fact were considered to be supplemental to each other and were made to match in these details. We find, therefore, amices of silk and of satin, embroidered and jewelled. That Bishop Riculfus, to whose last will and testament reference has already been made, bequeathed to his church four amices enriched with gold; and the inventory of S. Paul's Cathedral in 1295 contains many amices, costly both in material and in work. Many of the linen amices, also, had beautifully worked apparels; which in this case were oblong pieces of embroidered silk, velvet, or other rich stuff, attached to the upper edge of the vestment, so as to turn back and make a handsome collar, yet still leaving the linen next to the skin of the wearer. As in the case of the alb, so here, also, the more primitive use is now again the custom, and the amice is usually simply linen, adorned, if at all, with some slight needlework upon the upper edge of the material itself. Amices with rich apparels were in use at Angers, and at Bourges, at the end of the seventeenth century; and some priests in

England have revived the use of the apparel to the amice, as they have also done with the alb.

The accompanying woodcuts show an ancient amice, enriched with a deep apparel of embroidery, first while being arranged, and then in its final position. It is put about the neck and tucked inside the collar of the cassock, the upper part being then raised over the head until the other vestments have been donned. It is then thrown back so that the apparel forms a broad collar to the chasuble. The simple linen amice, without apparel, is rolled back over the stole before the putting on of the chasuble.

This vestment is generally supposed to have been the original of the modern use of white linen about the neck, whether as collar only or as collar and white tie, by the clergy. In the Tudor period it was transformed into a neckcloth with long ends, which in course of time became the clerical bands once universally worn, and still, though seldom seen, to some extent part of the official dress of the English clergy. Bands are mentioned as forming, with cap, gown, and tippet, their costume out of doors as early as 1566, at which date they are so spoken of in a letter from Miles Coverdale and others to Theodore Beza. The broad ends were afterwards dropped, except for ceremonious occasions, and only the wide neckcloth remained; which within present memories has become, first a white collar with a necktie, and then the clerical collar as now usually worn, or the band or strip of linen stretched over a black stock, not infrequently used.

AMICE (from Pugin's Glossary of Costume).

In France bands of the older shape are still worn, but of black or dark blue material edged with white. Barristers still wear in England a similar arrangement of white lawn or linen, but with longer ends than the clerical bands. They formerly formed part of the dress of graduates at the universities, and are retained at some of the public schools, as at Christ's Hospital, and among the scholars at Winchester. Vicars, choral and singing men, who anciently were sometimes vested in amices, subsequently wore bands over their surplices.

These "linen fragments which some bind about their necks," as the Hereford Statutes of 1630 call them, are derived by some from the broad collars worn by all classes in the Tudor period. These were certainly sometimes called bands; while the Oxford University Statutes on the other hand, name the bands *collare*. Taylor, the Water Poet, says

> "The eighth Henry, as I understand,
> Was the first prince that ever wore a band."

The derivation from the amice is, however, the one most usually accepted as regards the use of the clergy; the lay bands have not improbably reached their very similar shape by developments from this wide lay collar.

CHAPTER VI.

The Vestment.

AMONG the somewhat numerous vestures worn by the clergy in their various ministrations, one garment, or set of garments, has come to be considered before all others as "the vestment," as being the chief one assumed by the priest in the highest of his offices. In the inventories of old church furniture it is not unusual to find such entries as the following: "A vestment of black satin of Bruges, and the things thereto belonging," as in a Hertfordshire inventory of the time of Edward VI.: or again, "A whole vestment for a Priest, with a Deacon and Subdeacon, of white damask with eagles of gold standing on books, bearing Scriptures on their head, and orfreys of a story of our Lady, with all things to the said vestment belonging;" this latter being part of the property of a gild-chapel at Boston. The vestment in the former entry, and the numerous similar ones, includes the whole suit worn by the celebrant at the altar other than those of linen, namely stole, maniple, and chasuble. The "whole vestment" of the latter quotation obviously embraces the necessary robes not only for the celebrant, but also for the assistant ministers at a High Mass.

The first Prayer Book of King Edward VI. uses the term, in a passage already alluded to, in a sense quite similar, when it orders the priest to assume at the time of the Holy Eucharist "a white alb plain with a vestment." A distinction is here made between the vestures of linen, and those of more costly materials; and having already considered the linen garments of the clergy, this chapter is to treat of the vestment in this latter sense. The following will therefore be included in it: the chasuble, dalmatic, and tunicle of the priest, deacon, and sub-deacon, the stoles used by the first two of these, and maniples by all the three.

The chasuble, by a yet further restriction of meaning, has sometimes been by itself called "the vestment," as in some lists of the ornaments of the ministers of the sixteenth century; the reason of such a limitation of the term being obvious, when we remember that the chasuble, as a large upper garment, is almost the only one which is really visible to the people in its entirety.

The word chasuble, or in its Latin form *casula*, means a little house, and was applied to this vestment because it was originally so ample as to cover the whole man. The name, however, is not found as the undoubted term for a sacerdotal garment until the beginning of the ninth century. It is frequently used of a cloak commonly worn by secular persons in times anterior to that date, and especially by persons of lowly rank. Hence in the sixth century the monks made the use of it one of the badges of their voluntary poverty.

A garment, apparently similar in shape to the secular casula, but more costly in its materials, was the *planeta*, and this name is applied to a vestment used by the Christian ministry as early as the Council of Toledo in 633. The word is derived from a Greek source, and refers to the wavy lines in which the borders of so loosely fitting a garment wandered about the person of the wearer.

Allusion was made in an earlier chapter to the ancient

cloak known as a paenula; and in this it is agreed we find the origin of both the planeta and the casula. The name paenula, however, does not seem to have been ever employed of the dress of the clergy; planeta being the accepted term until the period, above given, when casula, or chasuble, became its regular designation in the West. The vestment is thus considerably older than its present name. For some time the two names existed side by side. In a charge ascribed to Leo IV. (A.D. 847) the vestment is called a casula, but Ratherius of Ravenna, who in 932 copies Leo, substitutes the older term planeta. In the year 831, Angesisus, giving to the Abbey of Fontanelle a number of vestments, is recorded as offering three casulae, and four "planetae casulae." It has been suggested, as an explanation of this latter double name, that, since originally the planeta was more handsome than the casula, it might still be used to describe a chasuble of more than ordinary dignity or costliness.

In France another name was at one time in vogue, namely *amphibalum*, or *amphimallum*, a word derived like the others from a cloak of similar shape in secular use. S. Remigius in 533 bequeaths to his successor in the bishopric of Rheims "a white Easter amphibalum." *Infula* was also a name for the chasuble in the middle ages. An old English term was *massa hakele*, or mass-mantle.

The primitive shape of this garment as a sacerdotal vestment was a circle with a hole in the middle for the insertion of the head. It thus fell in wide folds almost to the ground in front and behind, and at the sides below the hands. The inconvenience of this form is at once obvious; whenever the wearer ministered in it, the sides had to be gathered up so as to free the hands, or were turned completely back, so that the lower edge rested on the shoulders. To obviate this difficulty an oval design was afterwards adopted, so that although the chasuble still reached the ground, or almost so, in front and rear, it barely reached the wrists in its other measurement. Subsequently the whole garment was made shorter and less cumbrous, although it retained its ample and graceful folds till a late date, and especially in England. The continental chasuble was gradually cut away at the sides to give more freedom to the hands and arms, until it has become two oblong panels of silk, broad enough to cover the front and back of the priest, and in length reaching about to the knees or rather less; and these, which are sometimes curved into a "fiddle-back" shape, are joined at the shoulders by a strip of the material only some few inches wide. The date at which this cutting process began, at least in France, is indicated by Sirmond, who, writing in that country, says, "The

EARLIEST FORM OF CHASUBLE
(from the Catacombs).

chasuble, or planeta, began to lose the fulness of the toga by its sides being cut away, in the memory of our great-grandfathers." Sirmond died in 1651. A relic of the days when the chasuble was a full and heavy vestment is left to us in the custom which still obtains for the deacon, or the server, at the Holy Eucharist, to raise the back of the vestment during the consecration prayer, and especially at the Elevation of the Host and of the Chalice; a custom, no doubt, very needful when the arms were confined and weighed down by a chasuble of the early mediæval type, but scarcely necessary now.

S. AUGUSTINE (*from Door of Chapter House, Rochester*).

Several of the illustrations in other sections of this book indirectly exhibit the shape of the chasuble. We have here, however, a series which marks its development. In the catacombs the primitive form is shown in the simple linen vestment falling evenly around the wearer, except where gathered up to give free action to the hands. The effigy of S. Augustine, of Canterbury, from the Chapter House door at Rochester, illustrates an early English form of chasuble, plain, ample, and flowing, reaching, in fact, almost to the feet. The design is much curtailed as shown in the curious brass of Sir Peter Legh, in Winwick Church, Lancashire. This gentleman, who died in 1527, lived for the greater part of his life as an honourable knight, but took holy orders some years before his death; he is represented, therefore, wearing the chasuble of the priest over the full armour of the knight. The later continental shape of this vestment is seen in Ruben's portrait of S. Ignatius Loyola; the sides are here quite cut away, leaving, however, a more ample front and back than is always the case with very modern specimens. The figure of Archbishop Stigand, on a subsequent page,

SIR PETER LEGH, KNIGHT AND PRIEST.

exhibits a curious type of chasuble, shown in several mediæval works of art; here, while the back keeps its ample size, the front from the level of the elbows has been entirely cut away.

When the Church began to adorn the vestments of her ministers with embroidery and jewels, naturally the chasuble, the most honourable of all, was not neglected. Broad orphreys were stitched upon it, covered with exquisite and elaborate needlework, in the production of which, according to Matthew Paris, the people of England were conspicuous. By a decision of the second council of Nicæa, in 787, the reproduction of human and animal forms was permitted on ecclesiastical vestures, and ample use was made of the liberty thus granted. A fine example is found at S. Apollinaris, at Ravenna, and is known as the Chasuble of the Diptychs. On the orphrey of gold colour, which runs down the front and back and round the neck, are the names and heads of thirty-five bishops, occupants of the see of Verona from its foundation to the middle of the eighth century.

S. IGNATIUS LEYOLA (after Reubens).

Amongst other famous chasubles that have been preserved is one illustrating the lay use of the garment till a late date, at any rate in certain cases; this is the green chasuble made in 1031, by Queen Grisella, for her husband

Stephen, the saintly King of Hungary, which is still treasured at Buda, and worn as a coronation robe by each successive sovereign. Two which formerly belonged to S. Boniface, martyred in 755, are to be seen at Mayence, and at S. Rambert-sur-Loire. The chasuble and other Eucharistic vestments of S. Thomas à Becket are preserved at Sens. Of this last an illustration is here given. It is slightly pointed in front and at the back, but in length still reaches so far at the sides that it must have been gathered up considerably over the arms in order to allow of free use to the hands. Its chief ornamentation is a somewhat elaborate arrangement of bands or orphreys, some needlework, including figures of angels, being added.

CHASUBLE OF S. THOMAS A BECKET.

The older form of the vestment was commonly adorned, both before and behind, with a **Y** cross, though the early English ones, as shewn in illuminated manuscripts, were frequently entirely without orphreys. See, for example, the exceedingly simple chasuble worn by Edmund Assheton, Rector of Middleton, Lancashire, as he is depicted in a brass in that church. Apparently each of the vestments in which he is clad has a narrow border of some kind on it, but beyond this they are entirely devoid of ornament. This is the more noticeable in this instance from the fact that Middleton was a valuable advowson in the gift of the lord of the manor, of whose family Edmund Assheton was a member; and moreover the date of his death, 1522, brings us to a period when splendid vestments were far from uncommon. Continental custom afterwards placed a Latin cross on the back, and a broad stripe in front—occasionally, and especially in Italy, a Latin cross was placed in front, as well as behind. The form and style of the decoration has never, however, come to be considered an essential feature of the vestment, and many handsome examples are to be seen covered with scroll-work in rich embroidery, after no definite and acknowledged pattern.

The position of the chasuble in the rubrics of the English Prayer Book has already been incidentally referred to. The book of 1549 bade the priest at "the Supper of the Lord and the Holy Communion, commonly called the Mass," wear a plain alb and a vestment, that is, a chasuble with its corresponding stole and maniple; but it also gave him the alternative of wearing a cope instead. The book of 1552 forbade the use of all these vestments, leaving only the rochet for a bishop, and a surplice for a priest or a deacon. The present book returns to the state of things in the first year of Edward VI.

The protestant feeling which urged the authorities to put all vestments under a ban, showed itself, as was natural, before the date of their formal condemnation. As early as 1528 a synod at Ely found occasion to order that no chaplain or priest in that diocese should presume "to celebrate in those unseemly garments (*togis indecentibus*) commonly called 'ruggid gowns.'" In the year 1550, among certain furniture sold from the church of S. Mary Hill, London, were "two copes, three vestments, and the cross banners," which brought in £6 13s. 4d.; also "two copes and seven vestments," which fetched £4; in 1551, Sir Thomas Wynsore, knight, bought from S. Mary's, Reading, "two white vestments for deken and sub-deken;" and from the same church "two men of London" bought for £14 13s. 4d. a number of ecclesiastical robes, including "a vestyment and one dekyng, and an old vestyment." The inventories of S. Paul's and every other Cathedral, as

EDMUND ASSHETON (*from a brass*).

well as most of the parish churches, reveal an incredible wealth of splendid vestments, costly in material, and beautiful in workmanship, almost every vestige of which was swept away. In some few cases altar cloths, pulpit hangings, and other similar church draperies were made out of them; but in most instances there can be little doubt that the work dedicated to God, and consecrated by sacred usage, was desecrated by profane employment. Becon, chaplain to Cranmer, in denouncing all vestments but the surplice in his "New Catechism," gives evidence of the richness of those in use in his time. "And because," he says, "that he which should minister at that gorgeous and sumptuous altar should answer in some point to the glory thereof, therefore it was devised that the minister also should have on his back gallant and gorgeous apparel, as an amice, an alb, a tunicle, a girdle, a fannel (maniple), a stole, a vestment, etc., whereof some were made of silk, some of velvet, some of cloth of gold; yea, and those garnished with angels, with images, with birds, with beasts, with fishes, with flowers, with herbs, with trees and with all things that might satisfy and please the vain eye of the carnal man."

In the question of vestments, as in so many other things, an energetic section of extreme reformers, who were constantly drawing inspiration and support from the followers of Calvin and Zwingle at Geneva, seem to have pushed matters further than either the people or the government really desired. Sampson, writing to Peter Martyr in June, 1560, thus piteously complains that neither the court nor the public was with them in their hatred of the old ritual—"Oh! my father, what can I hope for, when the ministry of the word is banished from court? while the crucifix is allowed, with lights burning before it? The altars indeed are removed, and the images also throughout the kingdom; the crucifix and candles are retained at court alone. And the wretched multitude are not only rejoicing at this, but will imitate it of their own accord. What can I hope when three of our lately appointed bishops are to officiate at the table of the Lord, one as priest, another as deacon, and a third as sub-deacon, before the image of the crucifix, or at least not far from it, with candles, and habited in the golden vestments of the papacy; and are thus to celebrate the Lord's Supper without a sermon?" About six years later than the date of this letter a book was published, by order of the Queen's Commissioners, in support of the use of the "surplice, cap, and other habits" by the clergy. Yet Grindal, in his successive archiepiscopal sees of York and Canterbury, which he occupied from 1570 until 1583, was diligent in enjoining the absolute destruction of "vestments, albs, tunicles, stoles, phanons," and every kind of Eucharistic accessory.

This is scarcely the place to discuss that revival of the use of the ancient vestments which the present century has witnessed in England; yet a movement which has spread so widely cannot be entirely ignored in considering the historic dress of the clergy. It must, however, suffice to point out that "the vestment," as our forefathers called the complete sacerdotal habit, is now worn in more than two thousand five hundred churches, so that it has again become the chief ministerial dress of no insignificant proportion of the English clergy.

Most that has been said concerning the destruction and revival of vestments holds good of the others as well as of the chasuble, although it is convenient to speak of the subject under the most prominent of them. It is time, however, to give some attention to the others.

In a solemn offering of the Holy Eucharist, the celebrant, or priest, is assisted by two ministers, who may be actually a deacon and a subdeacon, or, as is more commonly the case, priests, who for the occasion take the work assigned to those offices. The proper outer habits of these, corresponding to the chasuble of the priest, are the dalmatic and tunic, or tunicle, respectively.

The dalmatic was a tunic with long sleeves, introduced from Dalmatia (whence its name) to Rome late in the second century. It is mentioned as a fact which attracted remark at the time that the Emperors Commodus and Heliogabulus appeared in public in dalmatics. As a secular dress, however, it soon made its way among those of higher rank, as is shewn by the fact that S. Cyrian, Bishop of Carthage, went to his martyrdom clad in a dalmatic beneath his byrrhus, or cloak, and over his linea, or linen tunic. The secular traditions of this garment have never entirely died out. John the Deacon, writing, about the year 875, the life of S. Gregory the Great, tells us that the saint, as bishop, and his father Gordianus, as senator, wore dalmatics, and an ancient picture, supposed to be a copy of a yet earlier original, exists, in which are the figures of the two thus clad, and with them Sylvia, S. Gregory's mother. At the present time a dalmatic forms one of the coronation robes of sovereigns in England, and in some of the continental kingdoms.

The earliest traditions of the ecclesiastical use of this vestment belong to the local Church of Rome. S. Sylvester (330, A.D.), decreed that the deacons of the Roman Churches should assume the dalmatic instead of the shorter tunic, the *collobion*, which they had formerly worn. From this time it seems to have been regarded as a mark of papal favour, which the Pope granted somewhat sparingly to the clergy of other churches. S. Cuthbert of Durham was buried in a purple dalmatic. Zacharius, Pope in 741, gave one to the Bishop of Vienne, and the privilege of wearing one was granted also to the Bishop of Orleans. Gradually the custom spread of bishops wearing the dalmatic as part of their habit, its use by deacons being restricted to Rome and to a few other cities, such as Arles, whose deacons had it conferred upon them in the sixth century, Pope Symmachus, in granting it, specifically speaking of such a practice as being "according to the fashion of the Church of Rome." Similarly, Stephen III., about 755, granted the privilege to the Abbey of S. Denys. By the ninth century, as we learn from Walafrid Strabo, most bishops had assumed the dalmatic, and many priests also wore it beneath their chasubles when celebrating the Holy Eucharist, a

EARLIEST FORM OF DALMATIC
(*from the Catacombs*).

custom which survived at Orleans until the end of the last century.

The full episcopal habit still includes the dalmatic worn over a tunicle, as an expression of the fact that the bishop sums up in himself the powers of the lower orders of the ministry. The accompanying figure of a bishop in full pontificals shows the ancient chasuble of wide proportions, over a rich dalmatic; another example is given in the brass of Bishop Stanley on a later page.

In Gaul, down to the time of Pope Adrian I. (772, A.D.), deacons ministered at the altar in alb and stole only; but about that time the use of the dalmatic by that order began to become general.

The tunic, or tunicle, is very similar to the dalmatic in shape, but shorter, and with sleeves reaching only a little below the shoulder; nominally it is the special vestment of the subdeacon, but as a matter of fact, even before the Reformation, all distinction of any importance between the tunicle and the dalmatic had been lost, at least in England, both being made with short sleeves, and reaching about to the knees. As shown by the numerous inventories yet existing of church furniture, the name of the former vestment had almost died out of use, and the dress of both deacon and subdeacon was spoken of as a tunicle. Frequently the tunic of the former is more fully adorned than that of the latter, the subdeacon's having two broad longitudinal stripes down the front and back, while the deacon's has broad bands connecting these stripes near the top and the bottom; but even this small distinction is far from universal. These stripes are the modern representatives of those clavi, to whose presence on the Roman tunics of the first centuries

BISHOP IN PONTIFICALS.

allusion was made in the introductory chapter. Convenience was doubtless aimed at in reducing the proportions of the dalmatic's sleeves, and the length both of it and of the tunicle; but another result attained by the process is the bringing of both of them back to a nearer resemblance to that primitive colobion, which was in use ere the dalmatic was known in the Church.

The earliest and simplest form of the dalmatic as a church vestment is seen in frescoes in the catacombs; it appears as a short linen tunic, sleeved, and adorned with two parallel stripes of a dark colour. The mediæval form, with its long sleeves, is illustrated by the figure of a deacon vested for Mass; the alb, with its square apparel, and the amice, turned down to form the collar, are shown, while over all is a dalmatic without orphrey or ornament. It is slashed open for a short distance up each side, to render walking in it easier.

DEACON IN DALMATIC (*Pugin's Glossary*).

Far more ornate is the Sicilian tunic, dating from 1143, which is also engraved here. Rich embroidery adorns the

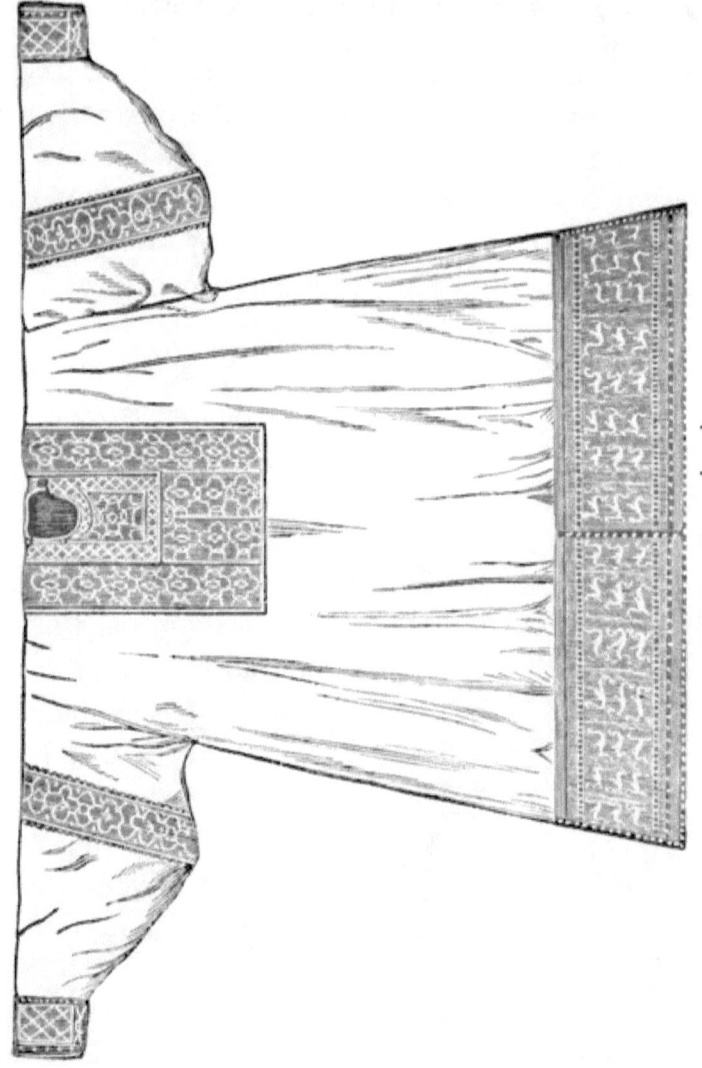
SICILIAN TUNIC (1143).

neck, the cuffs, and the bottom of the vestment, and there are bands similarly worked around the middle of the full sleeves.

Several dalmatics and tunicles, probably of the fourteenth century, are preserved at Spires, and in England some few ancient vestments have escaped destruction. At Salisbury is a green and gold chasuble of the sixteenth century; at Madeley are two of the fourteenth, and at S. Mary's, Oscott, are some ancient dalmatics and tunicles formerly at Waterford. A few fragments, these, from the great store of wonderful needlework once possessed by the English Church. One inventory recounts twenty-three tunicles at Canterbury alone, and another twenty-seven at S. Paul's.

In the Eastern Church the chasuble, there called *phaenolion*, is, like the Western vestment, a form of the early paenula, but with characteristic oriental conservatism, it has maintained far more nearly its original form. It is still a wide and flowing garment, which has to be gathered up to give free use to the hands. A variety of it, called *polystaurion*, from the fact that it is covered all over with little crosses, is one of the insignia of the episcopate. The dalmatic and tunicle are unknown in the East, the assistant ministers wearing a stoicharion (or alb) merely, with, in the case of deacons, a stole. The *sakkos* is a close-fitting garment with sleeves, not unlike a dalmatic, which is the upper vestment peculiar to metropolitans, although in Russia bishops generally have taken to the use of it.

The figures of two eastern saints give us good examples of the *Phaenolion* and the *Sakkos*. The first is seen to be a long plain chasuble in which the priest is completely muffled, and which requires to be rolled up over the arms to a considerable extent before the hands can be used. The *sakkos* is a more compact and less clumsy vestment, which for convenience in donning and doffing is open at the sides, and tied up with laces or ribbons when on. This figure illustrates also some others of the Eastern vestments to which reference will be made later.

The name stole originally described a loose robe worn by the ancients, and in this sense it is still used by English poets; thus Milton pictures Melancholy (Il Penseroso, v. 35) as having

"A sable stole of Cypress lawn
Over her decent shoulders drawn."

How the name has come to be applied to the scarf-like vestment now so called has not been definitely agreed upon by authorities in ecclesiastical etymology. The word is used in the Vulgate version of the Scriptures in most of those passages in which the authorized English translation has "robe." Thus the Levites are described as clad in stoles when conducting the sacred Ark to Jerusalem, and the saints in the Book of Revelation are "clothed in white stoles." These and similar passages would no doubt have an influence on the minds of mediæval churchmen, and we are not surprised to find the priestly habit as a whole occasionally spoken of under this term. It is thus that S. Isidore of Seville (died A.D. 636), alludes to the robes of the Levitical priesthood. That a name once applied to the whole should afterwards be exclusively used of a part, is not without illustrations in the history of language.

Amalarius, bishop of Metz, is one of the first to refer to this scarf under the name of stole, in a treatise on the Christian vestments written about the year 824. A work at one time ascribed to the learned Alcuin, who died in 804, comparing the official dress of the two dispensations, also uses the word stole in the modern sense; but it is agreed now that the work does not owe its existence to that great Englishman, nor can it be dated earlier than the year 1000 A.D.

The stole, however, was in use before this under the name of *orarium*, a name which implies its purpose, which was to wipe the face; it was in fact a primitive handkerchief. This was an ordinary article of dress amongst Roman gentlemen of the first Christian ages, and is more than once referred to by writers of her time. S. Jerome, for instance, reproving persons for an affected humility of garb, points out the folly of going without so decent a thing as a sudary or orarium, while at the same time the purse is well filled. Some ancient writers have derived the word orarium, not from *os* the face, but from *hora*, meaning hour; on the ground that the deacons of the primitive Church signalled with it to the priest the proper time for commencing the several portions of the liturgy. The orarium had, however, already been in use amongst the heathen as a signal, quite apart from any idea of specified times. The Emperor Aurelian (270 A.D.), distributed oraria among the people, that they might therewith wave their approbation in the

S. GERMANUS IN SAKKOS.

circus. The former derivation is usually accepted, although it is admitted that the deacon used his stole in the manner alleged; and an analogous custom is said by Isaac Casaubon, a well-known writer of the sixteenth century, to have existed among the Jews, an attendant standing beside the reader of the Law in the synagogue and indicating to the congregation by means of a sudary, or handkerchief, when they were to respond.

The earliest stoles, or oraria, therefore were, like the other vestments, not ecclesiastical in origin; and, like most of them, they were in their first form of linen. One of the first notices of them, as garments worn by officiating clergy, is in a decree of the Council of Braga in 562, which forbids deacons so to wear their oraria that they are concealed beneath their tunics, and the deacon cannot be distinguished from the sub-deacon. The fourth Council of Toledo in 633 bids the deacon to wear his orarium on the left shoulder, that the right arm may be more free for his duties. Another council at Braga in 675 ordains that the priest should wear it round his neck and crossed upon his breast. By this time it is consequently obvious that it was accepted as a matter coming within the scrutiny and control of the Church,

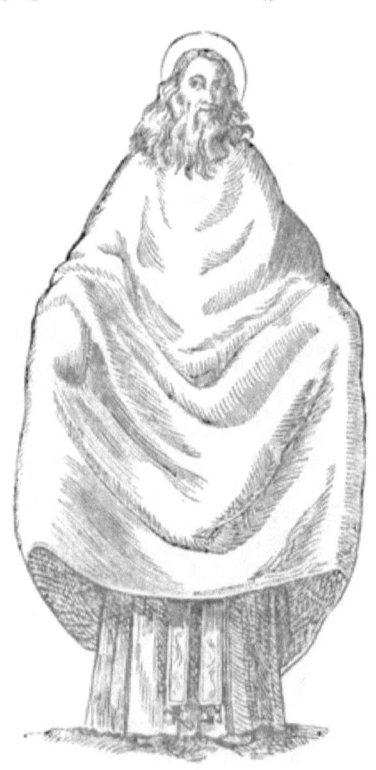

S. SAMPSON IN PHAENOLION.

Indeed that which was worn at first simply for use was already becoming an ornamental appendage to the ministerial costume; for that same Council of Toledo just quoted, thought it right to direct that the deacons' oraria must be plain, without adornment of colours or of gold.

In the eighth century the stole had so far established its position among the vestments, that priests and deacons were solemnly invested with it at ordination. The Pontifical of Egbert, Archbishop of York (732-766), and that of S. Dunstan, Archbishop of Canterbury (954-988), contain addresses to those ordained on the putting on of the stole. This practice did not become general on the Continent quite so early in the case of priests, the Pontifical of Soissons, about the end of the eleventh century, being the earliest to include it.

By that time the name orarium had given place to that of stole. Rabanus, writing about 819, speaks of "the orarium, which some call a stole"; while that alleged work of Alcuin, referred to above as having been really written by another hand in the eleventh century, in enumerating the vestments of the priesthood mentions this one by the name of stole only. It seems evident that the name, arising early in the ninth century, had come into common use by the eleventh.

Perhaps we may assume that the gradual rise of the more dignified name, and the discarding of the one which marked its first humble purpose, mark also the period at which the stole was losing its early simple form of a long linen napkin, and was becoming the rich vestment of the later time. In the seventh century we have seen that the Church insisted on the plainness of the stole, implying that such was still its common fashion, but that a tendency to decorate it was arising. The effort to check the development was unavailing, for in the will of that Bishop Riculfus, which has already been more than once quoted, and which is dated 915, we read of stoles adorned with gold and bells; and others equally ornate are spoken of at that period, or very little later. The early mediæval stoles were long, and of almost, if not quite, the same breadth throughout; the later Continental tendency has been to shorten them, while at the same time widening the ends. Three crosses are usually embroidered on them, one in the middle, and one at either end; the ends are fringed, and the whole is often elaborately embroidered. In mediæval times it was not uncommon to adorn them, as we have seen copes were sometimes adorned, with little bells. Two English stoles, dating from the reign of Henry VI., have been preserved, and are now in the possession of Lord Willoughby de Broke. The stole of S. Thomas à Becket, preserved with others of his vestments at Sens, is a good example of the mediæval type. It is embroidered throughout, and in the place of fringe, has three tassels at either end. In recent years this antique stole has been used as a model for imitation, and several have been made like it for use in England.

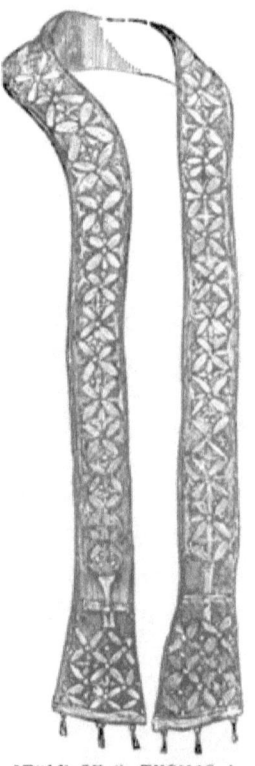

STOLE OF S. THOMAS A BECKET.

None of those vestments, which, after the Reformation,

fell into disuse in England, have been so generally restored as the stole. This is undoubtedly largely due to the fact that the people never ceased to be familiar with a clerical habit very similar in appearance; namely, that very greatly curtailed example of the black monastic cope which, as has been pointed out, still exists as the canons' scarf. About the time of Queen Anne this scarf was also assumed by the private chaplains of noblemen, and thus both in cathedral cities and in the country it was often seen. This will account both for the ease with which the stole has been generally introduced, and for the fact that for a long time after its re-introduction it was uniformly black in colour, like the scarves referred to. In the early days of its revival, however, liturgiology was little understood by most English priests, and as a consequence the black stole was worn, not only in those offices that, by ecclesiastical rule and tradition, demanded it, but for all services indiscriminately. Thus it is still a common thing at a confirmation, or other service at which a number of clerics are present, to see a long procession of priests, who have assumed stoles as if they were part of the invariable habit of their order. For this there is no authority, ancient or modern.

The Greek deacon wears a stole very like the type known in the West. It is still called *orarion*, or *horarion*, and is worn over the left shoulder; the deacon in the West, however, gathers the loose ends and fastens them beneath his right arm, while he of the East suffers them to fall down his left side before and behind. The priest's stole in the Greek Church is called *epitrachelion*, "a garment worn on the neck," and consists of a broad strip of material, with a hole at one end for the insertion of the head. There is no question but that these both have a common origin with the Western stole, and a well-defined seam down the middle of the epitrachelion plainly shows that its original shape was similar to that of the others.

The stole, having become, in the way described, a silken and embroidered vestment, was no longer serviceable for the useful purpose for which it was at first worn. Yet the need of some handkerchief was felt, when the priest, robed in full vestments, was unable to reach the pocket which might be in his habit; and an early conciliar canon forbidding the use of two stoles, suggests the question whether some clerics may not, at the transitional period, have worn one for ornament and another for use. The perception of this need gave rise to the use of the maniple.

This vestment, which in shape is like a very small stole, stitched together so that it may be carried, without fear of falling off, on the left fore-arm, has been variously called *mappulla* (napkin), *mantile* (a handkerchief), and *fanon*, or *phanon*, corrupted often into fannel (a flag or ensign). It was originally like the stole, whose place it took, simply a linen kerchief for wiping the hands and face. Rabanus mentions it early in the ninth century; it was, however, in use considerably earlier in Rome, and the custom of wearing it spread thence, much as that of the stole had done. S. Gregory gave the deacons of Ravenna leave to don it, but only when in attendance on the bishop. At first the maniple was carried in the left hand, and we see it thus represented in old paintings; for example, in an eleventh century Italian fresco, which represents S. Clement saying mass, having, with the other appropriate vestments, a maniple hanging across his left hand. And in the Bayeux tapestry, Stigand,

Archbishop of Canterbury, is seen officiating at the coronation of Harold, holding a maniple in that way. This arrangement must soon have been found exceedingly inconvenient, and so the maniple was fastened together a little from the ends, and slipt over the left wrist. It is worn always on that arm, for the obvious reason that the right hand is to be left as free as possible for the service of its ministry. By the end of the ninth century, priests and deacons had very generally assumed the maniple, but it was not allowed to subdeacons until the eleventh.

But the maniple, once come into general use, soon began to be treated as the stole had been before it. From linen, it became silk or velvet, and embroidery and gold were lavished on it, until it, too, became a recognized vestment. At King's College, Cambridge, in 1453, was a maniple "of white sarcenet, streaked with gold." At Peterborough were some adorned, like some of the mediæval copes and stoles, with golden bells. Thus, once more, by a rather ill-judged application of devotion, the passion for enriching everything which was used in divine worship, rendered the maniple unsuitable for the office for which it was first made.

The Eastern Church has no maniple. Its place is, however, filled, to some extent, by the *epimanicia*, a pair of cuffs, which are tied with strings on to the wrists. In appearance they are, perhaps, more nearly allied to the apparels on the sleeves of mediæval albs.

Before closing this chapter, one word may be said of another vesture, which is not included in the general meaning of "the vestment," but is, nevertheless, most appropriately named here, from the fact that in use it is closely associated with those just discussed. This is the humeral veil, a broad piece of silk, or other costly material, which is assumed by the subdeacon during part of the Eucharistic service. As its name implies, it is worn over the shoulders, and in the folds of it the wearer holds the paten and chalice, as he

ARCHBISHOP STIGAND *(Bayeux Tapestry).*

brings them to the altar, and afterwards the paten until it is required by the priest. The priest uses this veil also at the service of Benediction, to muffle the foot of the monstrance while he is holding it; the object in each case being the same, to prevent the hands of the ministers from touching the sacred vessels. A canon of the Council of Laodicea, in the year 314, bids the subdeacon "bring the altar vessels to the deacon, but not touch them at the celebration." This vestment, an earlier name for which was *velum subdiaconale*, or subdeacon's veil, was probably, like others used at the Eucharist, originally of linen. The use of this was probably suggested by the divine command in the Book of Numbers (iv., 15): "When Aaron and his sons have made an end of covering . . . all the vessels of the sanctuary . . . the sons of Kohath (Levites) shall come and bear them, but they shall not touch any holy thing lest they die."

CHAPTER VII.

Miscellanea.

HAVING considered the most commonly used vestments of the clergy separately, it may be useful before going further to briefly summarize their use.

The cassock, we have seen, is the ancient, and still the recognized, clerical habit or coat, over which all ministerial vestments are worn. For all services, other than the Eucharist, the surplice or cotta, or in the case of a bishop the rochet, is the proper robe; over which for the sacramental offices and in preaching, the priest wears a stole, and in processions and certain solemn services, according to ancient usage, a cope. For the Holy Eucharist he assumes the amice about his neck, then the alb with its girdle, and the stole crossed upon his breast and kept in place by the ends of the girdle; the maniple is placed upon the left arm, and finally the chasuble is put on over all. The deacon is similarly vested save that the stole is placed on the left shoulder and fastened under the right arm, and a tunicle or dalmatic is worn instead of the chasuble, while the subdeacon is clad like the deacon except that he uses no stole at all.

The vestments which are severally characteristic of the various orders in the sacred ministry below the episcopate are illustrated in an interesting manner by the story of the degradation of William Sawtre, convicted as a Lollard in February, 1400. The accused, in full sacerdotal vesture, was presented before the Archbishop of Canterbury and the

Bishops of London, Lincoln, Hereford, Exeter, S. David's, and Rochester, in S. Paul's Cathedral. The chalice and paten were then taken out of his hands, and the chasuble stript from him, as a sign of his degradation from the priesthood; the book of the Gospels and the stole were removed, to show that he was no longer to be considered a deacon; and the divesting him of the alb and maniple bereft him of the office of subdeacon. Various church vessels and implements were then put into his hands and taken away again, in token of his degradation from the several minor orders of acolyte, exorcist, and reader; and finally the removal from him of the keys of the church and the surplice, by depriving him of the post of ostiary, or doorkeeper, destroyed the last shred of the ecclesiastical character attaching to him. His tonsure was then shaved off, and a layman's woollen cap was put upon his head.

Further we have noted that the same primitive costume has given us, by slightly different developments, both the Church vestments and the secular attire of the clergy. The clerical coat and vest being merely abbreviated forms of the cassock, the cloak a modified cope, and the white tie or collar probably a modified amice.

Several articles of dress, however, having points of historical interest about them, have not been touched upon in the preceding chapters. It is proposed therefore to gather up in this place a number of them which can not easily be classified.

In mediæval days it became usual, in view of the authority and dignity of the episcopal throne, to be precise in the case of bishops as to some minor portions of dress, of which little notice was taken in the case of other ecclesiastics. In the time of S. Gregory the Great shoes of the kind called *compaga*, which had been used especially by persons of senatorial rank, were reserved as a peculiar privilege for the clergy of Rome. Rabanus Maurus, the pupil of Alcuin, and Archbishop of Mayence, is however the first to count shoes, or more strictly sandals, among the characteristic marks of clerical dress. His treatise "*De Institutione Clericorum*" dates from the year 819, and it was in that century that sandals came to be reckoned part of the episcopal habit, black shoes having been usually worn before that time. A pair of sandals, once the property of Bishop Lynwoode (died 1446) is in the British Museum. By the end of the tenth century abbots, especially those that were exempt, began to seek permission to assume this, as well as other portions of the episcopal dress. The Abbot of S. Vincent, Metz, was one of the first to obtain the privilege, but others soon followed; and in the fourteenth century sandals of the episcopal type formed a regular part of the official dress of exempt abbots. The ordinary monastic sandal was fastened with a latchet, which was wanting in those worn by the higher orders. Priests were forbidden to say Mass in sandals.

S. Ivo, the pupil of Lanfranc, and bishop of Chartres, who died in 1115, is the first to mention the bishop's *caligae*, or leggings. He describes them as being of linen and reaching up to the knee. In later times they were called *tibialia*, and were made of silk. The boots worn by doctors of divinity in mediæval universities buttoned up the side, and both they and the episcopal gaiters as now worn, probably derived their origin from the caligae.

Boots are said to have been introduced by the Benedictines. The Franciscan friars, who to the last preserved more of the primitive simplicity of their saintly founder than most of the other orders, went bare-foot, or wore only rough sandals.

From shoes to gloves is a natural step. Honorius, a writer who flourished in the middle of the twelfth century, but of whom little is known, counts these as part of the appropriate dress of a bishop. *Chirothecae* was the recognized name for them. Frequently they were handsomely embroidered, with the arms of the diocese, or some sacred design on the back. A pair belonging to a bishop of London in the fourteenth century was worked in gold and enamel, and was valued at five pounds of the money of the time. The effigy of John de Shepey, Bishop of Rochester from 1352 until 1362, has a fine pair of these official gloves. A handsome pair, which belonged to William of Wykeham, is preserved at New College, Oxford. These gloves are of red silk, richly embroidered on the backs and round the gauntlets in gold. The effigy, already referred to, of Robert Pursglove, Suffragan-Bishop of Hull, which is found on a brass in Tideswell Church, supplies a good example of episcopal gloves; in this case the backs seem to be jewelled, and the gauntlets are very wide, ending in tassels. Similar gloves are seen also on the brass of Bishop Stanley at Manchester

GLOVES OF WILLIAM OF WYKEHAM.

A curious custom existed in England in the early part of this century, and in not a few cases down to quite recent years, namely, for the clergy to wear kid gloves in church, and especially while preaching. The habit is happily now quite obsolete. In this connection it is also interesting to note that in the sixteenth century, strange as it may seem to us in the nineteenth, it was thought irreverent to receive the Blessed Sacarament with bare hands, and it was customary in consequence for the laity to communicate gloved. Becon, Cranmer's Chaplain, notices the practice in his "Short Catechism." The old use was to hold a linen cloth before the communicants, beneath which they placed their hands on receiving the Blessed Sacrament, so as to catch any particle that might fall; it was perhaps the

ROBERT PURSGLOVE, SUFFRAGAN BISHOP OF HULL, TEMP. MARY *(Brass at Tideswell, Derbyshire).*

discontinuance of this practise, together with the tradition of the covering of the hands, which suggested the gloves.

The episcopal ring, the putting on which, together with the delivery of the crozier, formed an important part of the investiture of a bishop, has more than once given rise to fierce debate between the Church and secular princes, who have endeavoured to usurp the right of bestowing it. Its use was early adopted, the custom being inherited from the days of classical Rome. The acts of the fourth Council of Toledo, held in 633, speak of it as one of the insignia of a bishop; and on the opening of the tomb of Agilbert, Bishop of Paris in that century, a gold ring, with a jewel engraved with the effigies of our Lord and of S. Jerome, was found on his finger. S. Augustine speaks of his signet, and no doubt it was at first used, not as a mere ornament, but as an official seal. Amongst ancient episcopal rings that have been preserved, are those of William of Wykeham (1367-1404), and Gardiner (1531-1555). S. Cuthbert's ring also is at Ushaw, and several of the cathedrals have antique examples, whose original owners are now unknown. At first this ring was worn on the left hand; Gregory IV. moved it to the right in 827. Its use is retained by the English bishops, but is unknown in the East, except among the Armenians, and the Syrian Maronites. A thumb-stall, or pouncer, was a handsome ring worn by a bishop on his thumb, after it had been dipped in holy oil, to prevent the chrysm from rubbing off on to his vestments.

The brass in Manchester Cathedral of James Stanley, Bishop of Ely from 1506 to 1515, shows him to us wearing a large ring on the thumb, and another on the third finger of his right hand. They are put on outside the glove, and, as the manner then was, between the first and second joints of the fingers. A letter of Winchelsey, Archbishop of Canterbury in 1310, proves that at that time the primate claimed as his own the official ring of every deceased prelate in his province.

The cross worn by a bishop on his breast, and hence called a pectoral cross, or *encolpium*, is an ancient ornament in the West. The one used by S. Cuthbert is still preserved at Durham, and there are records of the use of such a one by S. Gregory of Tours, and S. Alphege. Many, but not all, of the modern English bishops wear the pectoral cross.*

A more important vestment is the pallium, or pall, worn by most western metropolitans, and by a few privileged bishops, to which special prominence has been given by the papal claim to the exclusive right of its bestowal, coupled with the

* See further the Author's "Cross in Ritual, Architecture, and Art," (Andrews, 1896), p. 39.

STANLEY, BISHOP OF ELY, 1506-1515.

assertion that no archbishop can lawfully officiate until it has been so bestowed.

The word *pallium* has been used by ecclesiastical writers in various senses. S. Isidore of Seville usually employs it with the general meaning of a garment, and speaks of the paenula, the lacerna, and other ancient cloaks or tunics all as pallia, adding a distinguishing phrase in each case. Pope S. Celestine uses it of the monastic cloak. Both Rabanus Maurus and Walafrid Strabo quote Pope S. Sylvester as ordaining that every deacon should wear on his left arm a pallium of woven linen (pallium linostimum), by which apparently the primitive maniple is meant. In Rome, in the first century, the word was used as an equivalent for the Greek *himation*, which was the cloak of the Eastern empire answering to the toga in the West—the main difference, it is alleged, being that the latter was circular, whereas the former was a square. It was thrown round the body, so as to leave the opening at the right side, the right arm being thus free, while the left was enveloped in its folds ; a brooch fastened it upon the right shoulder. So plain and simple a garment was it at first that Diogenes and his fellow cynics adopted it as their chosen garb, but in the later empire it became in an enriched form the robe of the Emperor. A mosaic of the sixth century in the church of S. Vitalis at Ravenna represents the Emperor Justinian assisting at the consecration of that church, he and his attendant nobles being robed in pallia of the kind described.

There was, however, another method of donning the pallium found in the sixth century, both in the East and in the West. The robe in this case was less ample, and was gathered about the waist, and turned over each shoulder in a way very similar to that adopted with a Highland plaid. The Arundel Society has produced facsimiles of ivory diptychs which illustrate this use in the case of Boethius, Consul of the West in 510, and Clementinus, Consul of the East in 513. From this pallium, it has been supposed, the *omophorion* of the Greek Church, and the archiepiscopal pall of the Latin, have been derived by that process of contraction and abbreviation which has shown itself in the case of so many vestments.

The former of these is mentioned as one of the episcopal insignia by Isidore of Pelusium, who flourished about 412, and in a manuscript of the tenth or eleventh century is represented as worn by all the bishops at the second Council of Nicæa. It consists of a long strip of woollen stuff, which is worn so loosely round the neck as to fall in a loop over the breast, the two ends falling down the left side before and behind. Isidore speaks of it as marking the bishop just as the stole does the deacon, and alleges that all bishops wear it to remind them that as under-shepherds they "must bear the infirmities of the flock." At the reading of the Gospel, however, it is laid aside, the Chief Shepherd Himself having then undertaken the guidance of His sheep. The omophorion of Archbishop Moses, who lived in the early fourteenth century, is still preserved; and the vestment is worn to this day, in a shape very little different from its original one, by all the bishops of the Eastern Communion.

The first Council of Macon, in 581, decreed that no archbishop should say mass without his pallium. From this it has been supposed that there was a Gallic pallium, possibly derived directly from Eastern sources, which the metropolitans of Gaul invariably wore in primitive times, a pallium distinct, perhaps, to some extent in shape, from the badge of papal authority, which latter may have also been in use in addition to the Gallic pallium, as it has been called.

The early form of the Roman pallium seems to have been similar to the Eastern one. It appears in a painting and a mosaic both already referred to. S. Gregory the Great wears it in the ancient picture in which he, his father, and his mother are all represented; and in that mosaic at Ravenna, spoken of above, it is seen on the shoulders of Maximianus, the archbishop. Frescoes also exist in the Catacombs, dating from the sixth and following centuries, in which are the figures S. Cornelius and S. Xystus, popes, S. Cyprian, and others, all wearing the pallium in the Greek fashion, with the loose ends hanging on the left side.

In later ages it assumed a more rigid pattern, and became a circle placed round the neck with long ends hanging from it down the middle of the robes in front and at the back. So we see S. Clement, vested for mass in a fresco in Rome of the eleventh century, where the pallium hangs almost to the bottom of the alb. In this shape it forms a Y on the front and back of the chasuble, and is very like the orphreys attached to that vestment in mediæval times. Such a pallium is seen on the figure of Archbishop Stigand in the Bayeux tapestry, engraved above. At the present day it is made much shorter, the pendant ends falling little further than the breast and the middle of the back.

The wool of which the pallium of the Latin Church is manufactured is specially prepared for its purpose. The lambs, two in number, whose fleece is to be used, are solemnly blessed on S. Agnes' Day in the church dedicated in the name of that saint at Rome; the wool itself being separately blessed on the Feast of S. Peter and S. Paul, after lying the preceding night on the altar of S. Peter. Before the eighth century it was embroidered with red crosses; it now has six black ones.

This vestment was originally conferred on metropolitans as a symbol of special honour and authority conferred by the Pope, but not as a necessary qualification for the archiepiscopal rank. Arles, for instance, claimed that dignity before the days of Pope Symmachus, who gave the pallium to Cæsarius, one of its archbishops. The Bishops of Bamberg and of Lucca received the unusual privilege of wearing it, the former in 1046, and the latter in 1057. S. Gregory sent a pallium to S. Augustine of Canterbury, and all his successors in that see, as well as the Archbishops of York, wore such a vestment down to the era of the Reformation. The Archbishop of S. Andrew's received a pallium in 1472, in token of his being made independent of the see of York. The papal authority was first admitted in Ireland in 1152, when, at the Council of Kells, the papal legate presented palls to the four Irish archbishops.

It is admitted that at first the pallium was given by the Pope in conjunction with the civil authority. S. Gregory says of himself that he sends one to the Archbishop of Arles with the assent of the Emperor, the reigning sovereign of the time being Maurice of Byzantium. And before this, Vigilius, when (about 545) he showed the like favour to Auxanius, another occupant of that ancient see, did so "as our most glorious son, King Childebert, has with Christian devotion, commissioned us (pro Christiana devotione mandatis)." An early papal decree bade every metropolitan come to Rome personally to fetch his pallium within three months of his consecration, a command which cost many archiepiscopal pilgrims dear, in spite of another decree of S. Gregory's, forbiding all officials to take any fee at the delivery of it. The See of Mayence is said to have been once put to the expense of 30,000 gold pieces in obtaining its pallium. The diocesan arms of Canterbury, Armagh, and Dublin, are still charged with a white pall with black crosses.

Pope Gregory XI. (1370) declared that no metropolitan could consecrate a church or a bishop, summon a synod, or do any official act, until he had received this insignia of his authority. If he be translated, both he for his new see, and his successor in his old one, must procure fresh pallia; and at death the vestment is interred with him.

In the days when ecclesiastical writers loved to find, or force, a parallel between the vestments of the Christian priesthood and those divinely ordained under the Jewish dispensation, namely about the eleventh and twelfth centuries, the pallium was often spoken of as the rationale, a name by which the High Priest's breast-plate was denoted. The parallel was certainly in this case too wide to be perceived by the ordinary mind; beyond the fact that each lay upon the wearer's breast the two had nothing in common. Under the influence of this feeling, however, a usage sprung up, local and transitory only in its life, of wearing an actual representation, more or less exact, of that Old Testament vestment. In the Church of the Passion at Moscow a leathern breast-plate was found in a coffin; the date is not given, but the example seems, in any case, to have been exceptional. In the West there are some traces of such a custom having at one time existed, but it was so far from taking root, that even the form which the rationale assumed is very doubtful. An inventory of Saltzburg Cathedral makes mention of a rationale of gold, set with gems, and suspended by chains of gold, the worth of which was computed at a thousand marks.

Another vestment once in use, but now practically extinct in the Western Church, is the *succingulum*, or surcingle. This was not, as the name would imply, an under-girdle, but an appendage like a maniple hung on to the girdle on the left side. It is mentioned under the above, or other names, such as *praecinctorium*, or *baltheus pudicitiæ*, in various manuscripts dating about the fourteenth century, as one of the vestments worn by bishops. At the present time

PALLIUM.

it is worn only by the Pope when celebrating a Pontifical Mass. The *epigonation*, or *genuale*, is a vestment used at the Holy Eucharist in the Greek Church, which may have a common origin with this succingulum. It is a diamond-shaped pendant from the right side of the girdle, hanging down to the knee, whence its name. It may be seen in the figure of S. Germanus on an earlier page.

CHAPTER VIII.

Colours and Mystic Meanings of the Vestments.

OCCASION has arisen more than once already to point out that the clothing of the primitive clergy was probably white in colour. In later ages, as we have also noted, the ecclesiastical rank of the wearer came to be marked by the hue of his habit, the pope wearing a white cassock, cardinals red, bishops purple, and priests black. The different monastic orders also chose their distinguishing colours; black, white, gray, or brown being those generally selected. In all these cases, the head-gear, whether cowl, biretta, or skull-cap (zucchetto), agreed in colour with the cassock.

Other vestments are invariably white even to the present day. The alb, amice, girdle, surplice, and rochet are all of white linen only, although at one time coloured albs, as we have seen, were not uncommon.

Those vestments, however, which are made of silk, or of more costly materials, are found not only in colour, but also varying in colour according to the service or the season. Copes, chasubles, stoles, dalmatics, tunicles, maniples, humeral veils, of these a well appointed church has several sets, to be used at different times according to their hues, as laid down by ancient rules.

The practice of marking the sequence of the Christian

seasons by using vestments of different colours does not seem to have arisen until about the end of the twelfth century; certainly before that time it was not general or systematic. At that time, however, Pope Innocent III. gave rules for the use of four colours by the church in Rome; namely white from Christmas to Epiphany, from Easter to Pentecost and on some minor festivals; red for Pentecost and the feasts of martyrs; green for ferial days; and black for Advent, Lent, and a few special days. Almost immediately one modification in these colours took place; Durandus in 1286, and Cardinal Cajetan about the same time, enumerate five colours, violet replacing black except on Good Friday, and at masses for the dead. The emblematic nature of this sequence of colours is so obvious as to scarcely need explanation, and renders them at once serviceable in the way intended, as reminders of the events commemorated by the various feasts and fasts. White, almost everywhere in the West a sign of joy, is used for the great festivals of our Lord; while black, the hue of sorrow, marks the day of His crucifixion, and the funerals of our friends. Violet speaks to us naturally of penitence; and red, the colour both of fire and of blood, reminds us of the descent of the Holy Spirit in "tongues like as of fire," and of the blood of the martyrs. And lastly green, the ordinary and prevailing tint of nature, is not unnaturally employed for days when no special mystery or person is commemorated. These colours have maintained their places with but little change to the present time; blue has at times been used as a variety of violet or purple; and the festivals of the Blessed Virgin, and of saints who were confessors rather than martyrs, are now marked by the use of white: but as a whole this scheme of colours has lasted for six hundred years over a large portion of Christendom, and is to-day widely observed in the Church of England.

The rules in force on this matter in this country differed considerably in the various dioceses in mediæval times. Even within the diocese of London the use of the Cathedral of S. Paul and that of the extra-diocesan Abbey of S. Peter at Westminster, was not in all points the same. It has become usual in some quarters to speak of the ancient English use in this and other liturgical matters under the name of Sarum, as though the rules and rubrics compiled, or revised, by S. Osmond for his cathedral and diocese of Salisbury, were accepted throughout the length of the land. The more carefully, however, the question is studied in all its details, the more evident does it become that this was far from being the case. Lichfield, Exeter, London, Wells, Lincoln and Westminster, as well as the archdiocese of Canterbury, all had for instance, their local sequences of liturgical colours: and in the north the other primatial see of York, also took a more or less independent line in the matter. A certain similarity, it is true, ran through all the uses, but identity was so far from being attained, that one cannot but conclude that it was never aimed at. The Christmas and the Ascension Day colour everywhere was white, and the same is true of Easter, except at Westminster and Wells, which used red; white was also unanimously accepted on feasts of the Blessed Virgin and all other virgins. Red was equally universal on the festivals of all martyrs, of the Apostles, and at Pentecost, except in this last case at Salisbury and Lichfield, where white was employed, and at Westminster, where yellow or green might be substituted for red. The penitential colour also was in most instances red, and as such it was used during Lent and on Good Friday, although black was the Lenten colour at Lichfield, and violet or purple at Exeter and in London. It is natural to suppose that those churches, at any rate, which could afford to provide numerous vestments and altar hangings, would have some of a more sombre shade of red for this season than those used for festival purposes. The old English uses recognized some colours unknown to the Roman sequence. Blue appears at Wells for S. John Baptist's Day and Michaelmas, yellow is of frequent occurrence, being generally used for the feasts of Confessors; brown also is mentioned. At Exeter a combination of all colours was allowed on All Saints' Day. Black, as on the Continent, was the universal hue for requiem masses. Those churches which could afford vestments of so costly a material as cloth of gold, used them, to the exclusion of any other colour, on high festivals. Sir Thomas Cumberworth in 1440 presented to the chapel of the Holy Trinity in Somerby Church, "one vestment of whole cloth of gold, and a corporax with a case, and all that needs the Priest to minister in for great Double Feasts and principal feasts." Vestments of similar richness were to be found anciently in most of the cathedrals, and in many of the more important churches. Red was recognized by English use as the colour for Sunday, unless it was superseded by the occurrence of some festival which demanded the employment of white; and no doubt this accounts for the fact that in almost all churches where one altar-cloth only is found, the colour of that one from time immemorial has been red.

The mediæval fondness for this colour of red in its liturgical sequence is to a great extent in harmony with the Ambrosian use at Milan, where also it was employed more frequently than in accordance with the Roman rite. The usages of several French dioceses, as for example, Sens and Le Mans, agreed also in sundry particulars with those in vogue in England.*

The Eastern Church, with that strong conservatism which is one of its leading marks, has preserved the primitive use of white far more than has been done in the West; in fact, it is the colour exclusively worn there, except at the penitential seasons, when violet is used.

The colours also vary in some cases for the several services, independently of the season; thus white is used for marriages, and baptisms, black for funerals, and violet for confessions. The colours of the vestments may be supposed to aim chiefly at teaching the people, by reminding them of the gladness or sadness, as the case may be, of the event or mystery that day commemorated. But a mystical meaning has also been drawn from each of these sacerdotal robes, which is intended specially for the instruction of the priest, a meaning of which he is reminded by a special prayer prescribed for his use as he dons each portion of the ceremonial vesture. Some few of these meanings have been incidentally noticed already. To what a painful degree of minuteness these garments have all been moralised, let this account of the cope illustrate; "It has a hood at the top, which signifies the joy above; it reaches to the feet, because it is meet to persevere in a holy conversation unto the end;

---

* For a brief but exhaustive treatise on the mediæval uses in England in this respect, see "On the English Liturgical Colours," by W. H. St. John Hope, M.A. London, 1889.

by the fringe is denoted the labour through which the service of God is effected; it is left open in front, because eternal life is open to the ministers of Christ who live holily."

Without attempting to follow such commentators through all the meanings which may be thus extracted from (or perhaps more truly, be forced into) every fold and stitch of each of the vestments; it will, nevertheless, be interesting to note in concluding our discussion of these ancient articles of clerical dress, some of the teachings which they have suggested to devout minds.

Two lines of thought have been followed in this matter; the various vestments have been considered as emblematical of the bonds, the robes of mockery, and other accessories to the Passion of Christ; so that the priest, about to offer that Holy Eucharist wherein "we do show forth the Lord's death," may feel that therein he is the representative to the people of "the Great High Priest." Again, these vestments have been given a metaphorical significance, reminding the wearer of those Christian graces and virtues with which the faithful priest should be equipped.

Taking the first of these two methods of interpretation, we are told that the Eucharistic vestments have the following meanings. The amice signifies the veil or cloth with which our Saviour's eyes were bound during His subjection to the mockery of His foes. The alb typifies the robe in which Herod arrayed Him. The girdle is the cord of the scourging, and the stole the ropes by which He was bound to the pillar for that torture. The maniple in the West, and the epimanicia in the East, speak of the bonds which fastened the sacred hands of the Redeemer. The chasuble symbolizes the purple robe with which Pontius Pilate invested Him. These meanings are for the most part those given by Cranmer, in a "Rationale" published by him, or by his authority, in 1543.

Different writers have taken different views of the divine graces of which these vestments might be considered emblematical. An early authority, John Miræus, prior of Lilleshall in 1403, makes the amice denote faith; the alb, purity; the girdle, chastity; the maniple, fortitude; the stole, humility; the chasuble, charity; and Cranmer, in the work just referred to, agrees with these in the main. The meaning given to the amice probably arises from its occasional use as a head-covering, suggestive of a "helmet of salvation." The stole implies humility from its likeness to a yoke, and also from its suggestion of bearing the cross when it is crossed on the priest's breast. The chasuble is charity as covering all. The alb and the girdle explain themselves. It may be that in ascribing fortitude as a meaning to the maniple the writers had in mind the same thought as that which is entertained in the Greek Church with regard to the genuale, namely, that it distantly resembles a sword.

The Roman Missal in the several prayers to be said while vesting, suggests a slightly different series of meanings; namely, by the amice is implied the "helmet of salvation;" by the alb, purity; by the girdle, continence; by the maniple, contrition; by the stole, immortality; by the chasuble, obedience, and the burden of the priest's responsibility.

In a similar way all the appropriate robes of the several orders of the ministry have been spiritualized, by an ingenuity which one cannot but feel sometimes to be strained, and even misplaced, in the minuteness of its application. The enunciation of broad principles to help to fix the mind of the priest when about to go to the altar, will often prove most edifying; to twist and torture every accidental detail of a vestment's cut or fashion into an allegory, can be productive of little good.

Thus, briefly, we have reviewed the history of the dress, secular and official, of the clergy. The greater part of our space has of necessity been taken up with an account of those richer vestments which the Church throughout the world has long dedicated to the highest act in her worship; and which the plain meaning of the rubrics of the English Church claims as part of her heritage.

The colour or shape of a robe may be, no doubt in fact is, a matter in itself of but little importance. But circumstances may give even to a trifle a position which exalts it almost into a principle. By the use of the ancient vestments of her ministers, for example, the English Church asserts in the teeth alike of Puritanism and Papalism, her claim that those ministers are the ambassadors of the King of kings; she sets forth also before the eyes of all the fact that not by preaching, or even by prayer, do we reach the highest act of earthly devotion to God, but that in the Christian sacrifice we pay Him our truest and most solemn worship; and finally, even by the use of these vestments, the Church of England asserts once more her claim to be an integral part of that One, Holy, Catholic, and Apostolic Church of Christ, whose four divine marks have been so sadly obscured, but not obliterated, by the evil passions of sinful men. The outward sign of the claim may be of little worth, yet by the consent of both friends and foes the inward insignificance is of vast importance.

Index.

Abbots, use of Episcopal Insignia by, 53, 109
Academical Hoods, 43-44
Alb, 61-65; In Edwardine Prayer Book, 65
Albi, Council of, 20
Almuces, 40-44; forbidden in England, 42
Ama'arius on the use of the stole, 97
American use of the Mitre, 55
Amice, 73-77
Amphibalum or *Amphimallum*, 80
Anagolagus, or *anagolium*, 74
Ancient Dalmatics, 96
Andrewes', Bishop, Hat, 47
Angers, use of Amice at 74-75
Apostles use of Levitical vestments, 8
Apparels, 63, 75
Archbishop's Mitre, 56; Pallium, 113-118
Arguments of Puritans against Clerical Dress, 23; against the surplice, 70
Armenian Amice, 74; Clerical Head-gear, 50
Assheton, brass of, 86-87
Augustine, S., on the *Casula*, 19; on early mitres, 49
Augustinian Canons, 20

Bands, clerical, 76, 77
Barbarian invasion of, 17; dress, 18
Beaumont, on surplices at Cambridge, 70
Becket, S. Thomas à, vestments of, 52, 64, 85, 101

Becon on vestments, 88
Bells on vestments, 32, 101, 104
Benedict, S., 18
Beverley, Percy tomb at, 74
Biretta, 48
Birrus, 13, 48
Black dress of Clergy, 15, 22; habits at funerals, 22; Gowns for preachers, 68
Bona, Cardinal, on surplices, 67
Boniface, S. on the *casula*, 19
Bonnet of Levitical priests, 3
Bourges, amices at, 75
Braga, Council of, 99
Brasses, at Eccleston, 33, 68; Manchester, 42, 68, 112, 113; Middleton, 86, 87; Winwick, 83
Breastplate, Levitical, 3, 118
Bucer on the square cap, 46
Byrrhus, 13

Caesarius of Arles, his use of the *casula*, 19
Calabres, 40
Caligae, 109
Calvin on clerical dress, 24
Cambridge, the surplice at, 70
Camisia, 62
Canon of English Church on Dress, 24
Canons' copes, 28; scarves, 29
Cantor's copes, 29
Cardinal's hat, 56
Carthage, council of, 62
Cartwright's gown, 36; opinion of the almuce, 41
Cassock, modifications of, 24; modern use of, 25, 26

Casula, 18, 19, 79
Cecil, Sir William, on surplices, 69
Chancellade, Rochets at Abbey of, 73
Changes in the chasuble, 81
Chasuble, 79-90; of the Diptychs, 84: of Becket, 85; of S. Stephen of Hungary, 85; In the English Prayer Book, 86
Chimere, 72
Chirothecae, 110
Chiton, 5
Chlamys, 27
Choir copes, 28
Church use of Hoods, 44
Cinctures, 66
Cistercian monks, 20
Clavus, 6, 13
Clerical collars, 76
Cloaks, Priests', 30
Coat derived from the Cassock, 24
Collar of Sables, Parker's, 42
Collare, 77
Collars, clerical, 76
College cap, development of, 47
Colobion, 19
Cologne, council of, 21
Colour of Primitive Robes, 8, 14, 15
Coloured Albs, 63; amices, 75
Colours, Levitical sacred, 3; Liturgical sequences of, 121-124; of almuce, 43
Compaga, 109
Constantinople, council of, 18
Copes, 25-35; introduced by Pope Stephen, 28; of Canons, 28; of Cantors, 29; shape of, 30; when worn, 30; great number of, anciently in England, 31, 32; bells on, 32; desecration of, 32; post-reformation use of, 33; at the Eucharist, 33, 34; meaning of, 39, 124

Conference at Hampton Court, 71; at Savoy Palace, 71
Conservatism in dress of clergy, 11, 17
Constantine, conversion of, 17
Cosin's cope, 33
Costume, Roman, 5
Cotta, 68
Councils and Synods: Albi, 20; Braga, 99; Carthage, 62, Cologne, 21; Constantinople, 18; Ely, 87; Lambeth, 21; Laodicea, 106; Liege, 72; London, 21; Macon, 115; Melfi, 20; Narbonne, 18, 62; Nicæa, 18, 84, 115; Oxford, 67; Soissons, 18; Toledo, 79, 99, 110, 112; Tours, 45; Winchester, 67
Court Dress of English clergy, 38
Cox, Bishop, on the surplice, 69
Cranmer, on meaning of vestments, 126
Crowley objects to the surplice, 70
Crown, name for the mitre, 49; for the tonsure, 49
Cyril, S., of Jerusalem, 9

Dalmatics, 90-96
Deacons' Stoles, 99, 102
De Foe on use of copes, 34
Degradation of Sawtre from orders, 107
Destruction of vestments, 32, 64, 70
Diptychs, chasuble of, 84
Doctor's hoods, 44
Dowsing's Visitation in Suffolk, 70
Durham, copes used at, 33

Early English surplices, 67
Eastern Churches, girdles in, 66; hats in, 48; use of colours in, 124
Eccleston, brass at, 33, 68

INDEX.

Edmund, Archbishop, on vestments, 67
Edwardine Prayer Books on vestments, 65, 78
Elizabeth, Injunctions of, 23
Elmet, vestments destroyed at, 70
Ely, synod at, 87
Emblematical significance of vestments, 12, 125
Encolpium, 113
England and the Pallium, 117
English clergy, secularity in dress of, 21; Mitred abbots, 53; Canons on the tonsure, 59; Episcopal rings, 112; sequence of colours, 122
Epigonation, 119
Epimanicia, 104
Episcopal use of Dalmatic, 91, 92; Shoes, 109; Gaiters, 109; Gloves, 110; Ring, 111
Epitrachelion, 102

Fannel, 103
Fannon, 52, 103
Fisher, Cardinal, 45, 49
Foreign Almuces, 43
France, use of black garments, in, 22; Mitred abbots of, 54; bands of clergy in, 77
Fulgentius, Bishop, his *casula*, 19

Gaiters, 109
Galea, 74
Gallic Pallium, 115
Geneva gowns, 36, 39
Genuale, 119
Germanus, S., on copes, 39; of Paris, on albs, 65
Girdles, 65, 66; Jewish, 3
Gowns, origin of, 35; as outdoor dress, 35; for preaching, 36-38, 68; Genevan, 36, 39; used by Nonconformists, 38

Giles's, S., Cripplegate, Brawl at, 70
Gloves, 110
Greek church enforces clerical use of black clothes, 22; its liturgical colours, 124
Gregory, the Great, S., and barbaric dress, 18
Gregory Nazianzen, S., on early mitres, 48
Grey almuces, 40
Grindal, Archbishop, on clerical dress, 23; gowns, 35; albs, 64; vestments, 89;
Growth of monastic system, 18

Hampton Court conference, 71
Harding on use of gowns, 35; clerical hats, 45
Hats in the eastern churches, 48
Hegesippus quoted, 8
Helmet, amice compared to, 74, 126
Heraldic use of pallium, 118
Hermits, 15
High Priest's breast-plate, 3, 118
Himation, 114
Hood, academical, 43, 44; of the cope, 29
Hooker on clerical dress, 24; the surplice, 70
Hooper on clerical dress, 23
Horarion, 102
Humeral veil, 104
Humphrey, Lawrence, and surplices, 69
Huntingdon, brass of, 42, 68

Influence of monasticism, 16
Infula (of mitre), 51; for chasuble, 80
Injunctions of Elizabeth, 23, 34
Innocent III., his sequence of colours, 121
Innocent IV., allows use of almuce, 40
Invasion of Italy by the barbarians, 17

Interest of clerical dress, 2
Ireland and the Pallium, 117
Italy, invasion of, 17; use of black dress in, 22

James, S., dress of, 8, 9
Jerome, S., on vestments, 7, 8
Jewel, Archbishop, on surplices, 69
Jewish vestments, 2; compared with Christian, 4, 32, 66; tiara, 57
John, S., his "golden plate," 8; tonsure of, 59

Kidaris, a mitre, 48
Kid gloves in church, 110

Lace albs, 64; on surplices, 68
Lambeth, synod at, 21
Loadicea, council of, 106
Laud's copes, 21
Lectures in Church, 36, 38
Legh, Sir Peter, brass of, 83
Leofric, Bishop, will of, 72
Levitical vestments, 2; worn by Apostles, 8, 9
Liege, synod at, 72
Limerick mitre, 52
Linea, 62
Linen vestments, Jewish, 3; Christian, 8, 51, 61-77, 99, 106, 109
Liturgical colours, sequences of, 121-124
London, synod at, 21

Macarius, robe of, 9
Macon, council of, 115
Manchester, brasses at, 42, 68, 112, 113
Mandion or *Mandyas*, 39
Maniple, 103, 104
Mant, Archbishop on preachers' gowns, 37
Mantile, 103
Mappulla, 103
Martyr, Peter, on the surplice, 69

Maronite amice, 74
Massa-hakete, or mass-mantle, 80
Meaning of vestments, 12, 39, 124-127
Mediæval secularity in dress, 20, 21
Meïl, 3
Melfi, council of, 20
Metaphorical meaning of vestments, 126
Middleton, brass at, 86, 87
Milton quoted, 40, 97
Mitre, of High Priest, 4, 57; Episcopal, called a crown, 49; Primitive, 48; used since the Reformation in England, 55; worn by Abbots and others, 53, 54
Moderators of Scottish Kirks, dress of, 39
Monasticism, use of, 15, 18
Morses, 31

Narbonne, Council of, 18, 62
Necktie, Clerical, 76
Neville, Archbishop, on surplices, 67
Nicæa, second Council of, 18, 84, 115
Non-episcopal use of Mitres, 53-55; of rochets, 72
Norwich, state of Diocese of, 69
Number of Vestments anciently in England, 31, 32

Oferslipe, 67
Offices, when the cope is worn, 30
Omophorion, 115
Open Surplices, 68
Orarium, 98
Origin of Clerical dress, 5
Orphreys, 31, 84
Outdoor use of Gowns, 35
Oxford, Council at, 67

Pallium (a cloak), 13; (archiepiscopal), 113-118

INDEX. 133

Paenula, 27, 80
Palmer, on Eucharistic use of cope, 34
Papal Regnum, 57; gift of the Pallium, 117
Parker, Archbishop, his almuce, 42; on hats, 46
Parkhurst, Bishop, 69
Parures on albs, 63
Paul, S., the cloak of, 9; tonsure of, 59
Peckham, Archbishop, on Vestments, 67
Pectoral Cross, 113
Pepys on the preaching gown, 69
Percy Tomb, Beverley, 74
Peter, S., tonsure of, 59
Phaenolion, 96, 99
Phanon, 103
Philosopher's Pallium, 13
Phrygium, 57
Pilkington, Bishop, on hats, 46; on the mitre, 55
Planeta, 79; *planetæ casulae*, 80
Pluvialis, 27
Poderis, 62
Post-reformation use of the cope, 33, 34; the mitre, 55
Polystaurion, 96
Pouncer, 112
Paccinctorium, 119
Prayer Book on Hoods, 44; alb, 65; chasuble, 86; vestment, 78
Preacher's gown, 36-38, 68
Precious mitre, 53
Presbyterian use of gowns, 39
Priest's cloak, 30; dalmatics, 91
Principle of vestments, 7, 10
Primitive shape of chasuble, 80
Puritan opposition to clerical dress, 23; to the surplice, 69, 70, 71
Purple worn by Bishops, 23
Purrus, or *pyrrhus*, 48

"Quarterly Review" on the preaching gown, 36

Rationale, 118, 119
Reasons for use of almuce, 41; of amice, 74; of stole, 98; of maniple, 103; of humeral veil, 105
Regnum, 57
Remigius, S., will of, 80
Revival of use of mitres in England, 55; of vestments, 89; of the stole, 102
Riculfus, Bishop, will of, 66, 74, 101
Ring, Episcopal, 111
Rise of Monasticism, 15, 18
Roman civil costume, 5; mitre, 51; sequence of colours, 121
Rufus, S., Canons of, their rochets, 73
Russian clerical head gear, 50

Sakkos, 96, 98
Sale of vestments, 87
Salisbury, synod at, 21
Sampson on vestments, 88
Sandals, 109
Sandys on use of gowns, 35; of hats, 46
Savoy Conference, 71
Sawtre, degradation of, from orders, 107
Scarf, Canon's, 29
Scarlet worn by Cardinals, 23, 56
Scotch kirks, moderators' gowns, 39
Scotland and the pallium, 117
Second Council of Nicæa, 84
Secular use of copes, 28, 30; rochets, 72; dalmatics, 90; oraria, 98; pallia, 114, 115
Secularity in clerical dress, 20, 21
Sequences of liturgical colours, 121
Shape of cope, 30; chasuble, 80; stole, 101
Silk albs, 62; girdles, 66; amices, 74

INDEX.

Sirmond on shape of chasuble, 81
Sleeves of rochets, 72
Soissons, Council of, 18
Square cap, 45-48
Stanley, Bishop, brass of, 112, 113
Stephanos, a mitre, 48
Stephen, Pope, and the cope, 28
Stephen, S., of Hungary, chasuble of, 85
Stoicharion, 62, 96
Stole, 6, 97-103
Succingulum, or *Surcingle*, 119
Suffolk, Dowsing's visitation of, 70
Surplice, 66, 71
Superpellicium, 66
Sylvester, S., on the use of the dalmatic, 90

Tertullian quoted, 9
Thumb-stall, 112
Tiara, papal, 56
Tibialia, 109
Toga, 6
Toledo, Council of, 77, 99, 100, 112
Tonsure, 57-60; called a crown, 49; effect on dress, 60
Tours, synod at, 45
Trullo, Council in, 18
Tunic, Jewish, 3; Roman, 5, 13
Tunicle, 92
Turner's, Dean, use of a square cap, 47

Uniforms, 1

Vakass, 74
Vestment, the, 78
Vestments, meanings of, 12, 39, 124-127; sale of, 87; in Edwardine Prayer Books, 65, 78

Warham's, Archbishop, almuce, 42
Westminster, cope at, 33, 34
White robes used in primitive times, 8, 14, 15; now used, 120-122; worn by Pope, 23
Wigs, effect on shape of surplice 68
Will of Bishop Riculfus, 66, 74, 101; of Remigius, 80; of Wyndhill, 21
Winchelsey, Archbishop, on the surplice, 67
Winchester, synod of, 67
Winwick, brass at, 83
Wolsey, Cardinal, 45, 47
Wolverhampton, copes at, 33
Wyclif, Wm., 45, 46
Wykeham, Wm. of, his gloves, 110
Wyndhill, his will, 21

Xystus, S., fresco of, 116

York, black funeral habits at, 22

Ziz, 4
Zones, 65, 66

www.ingramcontent.com/pod-product-compliance
Lightning Source LLC
Chambersburg PA
CBHW030356170426
43202CB00010B/1393